Why Americans Don't Vote

WHY AMERICANS DON'T VOTE

Turnout Decline in the United States 1960–1984 _____

RUY A. TEIXEIRA

CONTRIBUTIONS IN POLITICAL SCIENCE, NUMBER 172

 Greenwood Press

NEW YORK · WESTPORT, CONNECTICUT · LONDON

35.00

9-17-90

Library of Congress Cataloging-in-Publication Data

Teixeira, Ruy A.
  Why Americans don't vote.

  (Contributions in political science, ISSN 0147-1066 ;
no. 172)
  Bibliography: p.
  Includes index.
  1. Voting—United States.   2. United States—Politics
and government—1945–   . I. Title.
JK1967.T45   1987   324.973   86-33585
ISBN 0-313-25532-6 (lib. bdg. : alk. paper)

British Library Cataloguing in Publication Data is available.

Library of Congress Catalog Card Number: 86-33585
ISBN: 0-313-25532-6
ISSN: 0147-1066

First published in 1987

Greenwood Press, Inc.
88 Post Road West, Westport, Connecticut 06881

Printed in the United States of America

The paper used in this book complies with the
Permanent Paper Standard issued by the National
Information Standards Organization (Z39.48-1984).

10 9 8 7 6 5 4 3 2

This book is dedicated to my mother, father, and brother, all of whom helped me in the best ways they knew possible.

It is also dedicated to Aage Sorensen and other people I worked with at the University of Wisconsin, who taught me how to do serious research.

Finally, it is dedicated to the American voter. In the future, may there be more of them and fewer of the people I studied for this book.

Contents

Tables

Preface

The American nonvoter, in most electoral contexts, is considerably more numerous than his or her voting counterpart. Yet the overwhelming proportion of research and commentary focuses on the American voter. The analysis in this book was undertaken as an attempt to redress this balance somewhat by studying, with advanced statistical methods, the behavior of the American nonvoter in the recent political past, 1960–1984.

This book originated at the University of Wisconsin, Sociology Department, between 1982 and 1984. At the time, the focus of the research project was the period of uninterrupted turnout decline in presidential elections between 1960 and 1980. Since then, not much has changed in the realm of American voter turnout, as turnout continues to be low, with only sluggish and occasional improvements. The original research has been expanded to include the 1980–1984 period, so this lack of improvement in the dismal turnout situation could be addressed.

It is worthwhile to say a few words here about the chapters that this book contains, and which ones might be of particular interest to different readers.

Chapter 1, the introductory chapter, sets the stage for the empirical study of turnout decline. In the process, many of the basic issues and facts about voter turnout are summarized. Thus, this chapter may be of particular interest to the general reader who wishes to become acquainted with the history and causes of voter turnout, as they are currently understood.

Chapter 2 explains the analytical strategy and statistical methods used in this study. The exposition here may be especially useful for those seeking a relatively clear and simple summary of how advanced statistical methods, such as probit analysis, may be applied to a concrete research problem in social science.

Chapters 3, 4, and 5 detail the various analytical steps that were taken to solve the research problem. The introductions and conclusions of these chapters contain information accessible and useful to the general reader. Beyond this, however, these chapters will probably be of interest mostly to the specialized reader who wishes to follow the steps in the research process and has more than a passing interest in multivariate analysis.

The last two chapters—chapters 6 and 7—contain much material of interest to the general reader. Chapter 6 describes how American nonvoters are different today than they have been in the past and addresses some of the current myths about nonvoters and their potential for partisan political mobilization. The obstacles to an overall increase in voter turnout are also discussed.

Chapter 7 presents some findings on the 1984 election and has some unusual and perhaps controversial things to say about the continued stagnation in U.S. voter turnout. The findings suggest that recent modest improvements in voter turnout do not show the way forward to high voter turnout levels, and, instead, by their very modesty, may indicate new weaknesses in the American voter turnout system. This is a matter of concern to the general reader, as it is, of course, to all Americans.

I should acknowledge here the help I received from various quarters in developing and completing this book. Certainly, the number of people who made a contribution prohibits me from making a complete listing. I would like to acknowledge my debt, however, to Aage Sorensen, Chuck Halaby, Erik Wright, and Rob Mare, who provided me with sound advice and concrete assistance at countless times in the research process. Also, there were other faculty members, including Jim Sweet, Pam Oliver, Jerry Marwell, and Maureen Hallinan, who helped me indirectly with the project by providing a "material basis" (employment, resources) from which the project could be pursued. In addition, the invaluable assistance of my graduate student friends—most especially, Mary Visher, Vern Baxter, Wayne Bigelow, Len Bloomquist, and Cindy Costello—who helped me get through the whole project in some semblance of psychological health should be mentioned.

I should also acknowledge some intellectual debts to people I have never met, but whose work influenced me greatly: Walter Dean Burnham for his general analysis of U.S. politics, Raymond Wolfinger and Steven Rosenstone for their work on the general determinants of nonvoting, and Paul Abramson and John Aldrich for their pathbreaking assessment of turnout decline in the 1960–1980 period.

Finally, while the people mentioned above bear a considerable amount of the credit for whatever merits the present work has, they must be exonerated for any of its shortcomings. These are the sole responsibility of the author.

Why Americans Don't Vote

1

Introduction: The Empty Polling Booth

Cherish . . . the spirit of your people and keep alive their attention. . . . If once they become inattentive to public affairs, you and I, and Congress and Assemblies, Judges and Governors, shall all become wolves.

—Thomas Jefferson

It has been called the puzzle of participation (Brody 1978). From 1960 to 1980, voting participation in presidential elections decreased monotonically from 65.4 percent of the eligible, voting age population to 55.1 percent (Burnham 1982, p. 101). This occurred despite two societal developments that led many observers to expect an increase in turnout: the easing of registration requirements and the dramatic increase in educational attainment, known to be a strong promoter of participation (Campbell et al. 1960).

This puzzle has occasioned much comment from scholars, journalists, public officials, and others concerned with American politics. There are two basic motivations for this commentary. The first stems from the view that the decline in turnout is symptomatic of a democratic society in a state of decay (Carter 1976; Hadley 1978; Burnham 1982). By this view, the essence of political democracy lies in the ability of the citizenry to select their own leaders through universal suffrage. The disinclination of a larger and larger proportion of eligible voters to exercise the franchise is thus seen as a malfunctioning of democracy. Somehow the system has developed in such a way that more citizens every election fail to politically participate in the easiest and most elementary form: by voting. This failure to participate means that the proportion of the population to which political elites must respond declines over time. This, in turn, allows narrower interest groups to assert their priorities, since proportionally fewer voters are necessary to influence an election, and gives political elites more freedom to do what they want. The result is a decay of the democratic link between governmental actions and popular wishes.

The other motivation is not quite so high-minded, generally being partisan in nature, and not rooted in concern over the future of the democratic form of government. Politicians of both parties and commentators from across the political spectrum (Perlez 1984; Rogers 1984; Walsh 1984; Americans for Civic Participation 1984) have noted the tremendous political potential of the growing pool of nonvoters. Given the large proportion of the electorate now present in this pool, the mobilization of even a small fraction of this group (78 million in 1980) could conceivably tip the balance in favor of one party or another. Exactly how to do this and who (if anyone) such mobilization would benefit are matters of controversy, but all agree that the potential is awesome.

It is difficult, however, to assess the meaning of declining turn-out, either in broad societal terms or within a narrower partisan political focus, when it is not understood why turnout declined in the first place. Filling this gap in understanding is therefore a worthy project, and the one to which this book is addressed. Specifically, this inquiry attempts to discover what changed in American society during this period that caused the turnout rate to fall to such an astonishingly low figure (not much better than one out of every two voters). This translates into identifying a set of factors that have pushed down turnout levels in the face of the counter-vailing forces (easier registration, increased education) mentioned earlier.

The first step along this road is to develop an analysis of why some people vote and other people do not. Such an analysis will provide a theoretical framework within which an appropriate research strategy can be considered.

Why People Vote

Looked at from one perspective, the amazing thing about voting is that everyone doesn't do it. It is, after all, a relatively low-cost activity, requiring little more than fulfilling some minor bureaucratic requirements and traveling to the polling place. On the plus side, the voter helps determine the nature of policies affecting his or her life by participating in the selection of policymakers. Yet everyone does not vote. Even at the beginning of the 1960–1980 period, about one in every three eligible voters didn't bother to cast a ballot. And in European countries, where turnout has traditionally been higher, turnout rates are by no means 100 percent, but vary widely between 70 and 90 percent.

There are two good reasons the perspective sketched above does not tally with the facts. The first is that voting, while a low-cost activity, is not a zero-cost activity. The costs of registering, finding out where the polling place is, and taking the time and effort to travel to it on election day are tangible, nonzero ones. In addition, there may be information costs, since not everyone will have easy access to the minimal amount of facts necessary to distinguish between candidates. For some people, this set of costs may seem large and not worth the trouble of absorbing.

The second reason has to do with the benefits obtained from balloting. Although it is true that the outcome of an election may have a substantial impact on a person's life, the individual citizen does not have to participate in the election to obtain these benefits. They are available to everyone, voter and nonvoter alike.[1] Theorists of voting have therefore pointed out that the worth of a citizen's vote is not equal to the benefits derived from a given election outcome, but to the product obtained from multiplying the value of these benefits by the probability that the citizen's individual vote will produce that outcome (Downs 1957). This "expected value" is the real outcome-related benefit of voting, and in most elections, it will be small, since the probability of a lone individual's vote affecting an election outcome is miniscule.

This makes it clearer why everyone does not participate in elections. The costs are nonzero and the benefits, in the expected value sense, may be so small as to be indistinguishable from zero. By this logic, it becomes surprising that anyone bothers to vote. This problem—the "paradox of voting"—has been duly noted by theorists of voting (Riker and Ordeshook 1968; Cyr 1975). The solution proposed by these theorists is simple and compelling: there are other benefits involved in voting besides its expected value. These benefits (formally termed "side payments" or "selective incentives") are primarily *expressive*. The citizen, by voting, expresses his or her sense of duty toward society, responsibility toward a reference group, commitment to a candidate, party, or cause, or any number of other feelings that are linked to the election or its outcome. It is these various ways of finding an election "meaningful" that motivate most people who vote to absorb the costs of balloting.

This view solves the paradox of voting and has been generally accepted among students of turnout. Implicit in the social psychological perspective of *The American Voter* (Campbell et al. 1960), where voting is ascribed to feelings of involvement and partisanship, it has become explicit in recent empirical studies of turnout (Wolfinger and Rosenstone 1980; Abramson and Aldrich 1982). It will be accepted here as a useful basic framework within which to consider the question of declining turnout.

Turnout in Comparative and Historical Perspective

The theoretical framework just outlined, while coherent and logical, is also too general to be of immediate use in isolating factors of potential relevance to turnout decline. The range of costs and benefits that could fit into this framework, and thus could conceivably be relevant to the 1960–1980 fall in voter participation, is too large to provide a sound initial basis for investigation. It is therefore necessary to explore the topic of turnout on a more concrete level, so that specific and detailed guidance for the research process can be obtained.

One way of doing this is to look at turnout in comparative and historical perspective. Turnout levels vary widely from country to country and have fluctuated dramatically over time within the United States (Burnham 1982). Developing an understanding of what factors have produced these variations may prove helpful in thinking about variation in turnout in the contemporary United States.

Turnout in Comparative Perspective. I turn first to the cross-national comparison of turnout rates (where the comparison is between the United States and other advanced industrial democracies). The most striking thing about this comparison is that turnout rates in these other countries are all higher—and usually substantially higher—than in the United States. While U.S. turnout rates were dropping from 65 to 55 percent in the 1960s and 1970s, rates in West Germany, Sweden, and Italy hovered around 90 percent. Rates in other countries were not quite as spectacular as in these three, but were generally over 70 percent and in no case were ever lower than in the United States (Burnham 1982; Hadley 1978).

The higher turnout rates in these countries may be traced to two fundamental ways in which their political systems differ from that of the United States. The first is that it is more difficult to vote in the United States than it is to vote in the other democracies (Wolfinger and Rosenstone 1980). It is harder to register, since bureaucratic requirements are more numerous, and the state takes no active role in registering people. It is harder to stay registered, since polling lists are purged for nonvoting, and those who move their residences usually have to re-register. And it is harder to actually vote, since election day is not a holiday, and absentee balloting is relatively difficult. In every respect, in fact, the legal structure of the voting process in the United States compares unfavorably with other democracies, in terms of its ability to facilitate voter participation. This makes the costs of voting higher in the United States and must therefore be part of the reason turnout rates are lower in this country.

The other way in which the U.S. system is different lies in the role of political parties. There are at least two aspects to this. The first stems from the fact that most other industrial democracies have some form of proportional representation, as opposed to the single-member district, first-past-the-post system that characterizes the United States. This allows the voter more opportunity to cast a ballot that reflects his or her beliefs without "wasting" a vote. The second may be located in the fact that parties in other countries play a more active role in commanding voter loyalty, as well as in mobilizing those voters to go to the polls (Lipset and Rokkan 1967; Duverger 1973). Both of these factors mean that the expressive benefits of voting, in party-related terms at least, are likely to be less in the United States than elsewhere. In addition, the second factor suggests that parties in other democracies play a cost-cutting role, through their voter mobilization activities, that is considerably greater than in the United States.

Thus it is apparent that in the United States, the roles of the state and the political parties are such as to make participation relatively difficult for the average citizen. The state, instead of keeping regulations and inconveniences to a minimum and actively assisting citizens in registration, makes qualifying to vote a time-consuming process contingent on individual effort. The political parties, instead of offering a wide range of alternatives and actively mobilizing voters to go to the polls, offer a fairly narrow range of alternatives and invest comparatively little energy in active mobilization of their political base.

This contrast may be summed up by saying that in the United States, voting is primarily an individual responsibility. The individual must surmount the bureaucratic obstacles necessary to vote. The individual must make sense out of a narrow range of political alternatives, within which his or her individual viewpoint may very well not be represented. The individual must, by and large, mobilize himself or herself to go down to the polls and cast a ballot. The individual, in short, has the burden of voting on his or her shoulders, rather than having that burden collectively shared, as in other countries.

Turnout in Historical Perspective. This point, about individual versus collective responsibility for voting, may be further illustrated by referring to the history of voting participation in the United States. It is not widely known that turnout levels in this country have, at different times, been both much higher and much lower than they are currently. The lowest levels occurred in the earliest years of the Republic. All American presidents from the first (Washington) through the fifth (Monroe) were elected with only 4 to 6 percent of the *eligible* electorate participating (that is, this low turnout rate does not reflect a population base including those not legally able to vote). The reasons why these turnout levels were so low are not clear, but there are at least two factors that students of the period agree were relevant (Hofstadter et al. 1967; Hadley 1978; Burnham 1982).

The first factor is that voting was a relatively difficult enterprise in the late 1700s and early 1800s. It was difficult to locate polling places and physically visit them, given the state of political organization and transportation facilities at the time. It was also difficult to find out the requisite information on which to base a voting decision, since newspapers were relatively hard to get hold of and tended not to have extensive coverage of national elections anyway. Thus, in early postcolonial America, the basic tasks of voting were hard for the ordinary citizen to handle.

Although the cost factor was important, it is generally deemed to have been less important than the role (or lack thereof) played by political parties at the time. Parties in this era did not have, nor did they attempt to cultivate, strong links to the rank and file of the electorate. They put forward their candidates and policies for the attention of those already interested in and aware of the political scene but made little effort to build up a sense of partisan identification and differentiation among the masses of the population. For this reason, the benefit-enhancing and cost-cutting effects of partisan mobilization did not obtain for most eligible voters in this time period.

It can therefore be seen that the average citizen was pretty much "on his own," in terms of overcoming the costs of voting and finding his way down to the polling booth. The costs were so high and the reasons for voting so uncompelling that most individuals could not attain sufficient motivation to vote. Here a system of individual responsibility for voting was remarkably ineffective in bringing people to the polls.

The voting environment changed dramatically with the advent of the Jacksonian era. Not only had the infrastructure of the country improved—better transportation, better physical organization of the electoral system, more widespread dissemination of political information—so as to facilitate participation, but the role of political parties underwent a sharp transformation as well. Led by the Jacksonian Democrats, parties reached out to the mass of eligible voters by raising important new issues, organizing on the local level, and using the newspapers to popularize their programs. As a result, turnout skyrocketed, reaching 57 percent in 1828 and

1832, and the 80 percent level by 1840. Evidently this partisan mobilization substantially increased the meaningfulness of voting for the average voter by allowing elections to be seen through the prism of party loyalty and identification. It also probably decreased the costs of participation through party informational outreach and get-out-the-vote activities.

Turnout in presidential elections remained high throughout the rest of the nineteenth century, sometimes over 80 percent, sometimes below that level, but almost never falling below 70 percent (the lone exception: 69.4 percent in 1852). The reasons why turnout consistently reached such levels are generally acknowledged to be rooted in the highly partisan nature of political campaigns during these years (a development initiated, as noted earlier, during the Jacksonian era). Not only the campaigns, but also the conduct of the elections themselves, were largely party matters (Chambers and Burnham 1967; Burnham 1970; Brownell and Stickle 1973). Parties, frequently organized into tight political "machines" on the local level, distributed vast amounts of partisan propaganda, held torchlight parades, distributed printed tickets that supporters could use for balloting, and generally orchestrated a voter's visit to the polling booth. This made voting both easy to do (especially given the lack of personal registration requirements at the time) and strongly expressive of a citizen's partisan commitments. The result was a long string of elections with high turnout levels.

The system of electoral participation that obtained during this period therefore took the burden of responsibility off the shoulders of the individual citizen and attached that responsibility to the political parties. Thus a basically individual system of responsibility for balloting was replaced by a much more collectively oriented one. This collective orientation probably explains why, despite some differences with the contemporary European situation— the range of alternatives, for instance, was narrower—turnout levels in post-Jacksonian nineteenth-century America are more similar to those in contemporary Europe than to those in the contemporary United States.

Turnout started dropping at the end of the nineteenth century, reaching the 60 percent level by the election of 1912. This downward trend (1896–1912) can be traced to the reforms of the Progressive era. The reforms that affected turnout can be divided into two groups (Wiebe 1967; Weinstein 1971; Burnham 1982). The first consisted of a variety of personal registration statutes that made the mechanics of voting more difficult for many Americans. These statutes functioned as barriers to mass participation by requiring individual voters to negotiate a series of bureaucratic obstacles in order to be permitted to vote. These changes were undoubtedly a factor in declining turnout.

The second group was composed of a series of structural and legal reforms (nonpartisan offices, at-large representation, direct primaries, ballot reform, recall and referenda, legislative regulation) that drastically damped down the partisan nature of electoral politics. This set of reforms also increased the costs of voting, since strong party mobilization had been important in getting people to the polls. In addition, these changes substantially reduced the meaningfulness of balloting for many citizens by depriving elections of their highly partisan coloration. Because the partisan link was such an important motivating force for American voters in the 1800s, it is reasonable to assume that the attenuation of this link made an important contribution to the fall in turnout levels.

In general, then, the collectively oriented system of voter participation ushered in during the Jacksonian era was replaced by one in which the individual voter had to take a great deal of responsibility for balloting. The individual citizen had to (a) surmount a series of bureaucratic obstacles in order to vote, and (b) formulate the expressive benefits of voting, once qualified, without the assistance of heavy partisan mobilization. Not surprisingly, this Progressive era system of electoral participation resulted in much lower turnout rates.

Turnout in post-Progressive era (1916–1980) America remained low, never reaching the levels attained before the Progressive era reforms. This is as would be expected, since there is little in the political history of these years that would indicate a return to a collectively oriented system of voter participation. The success of this system in promoting turnout varied from election to election but, interestingly enough, attained the best results in the era immediately preceding the period under study (1952–1960). These three contiguous elections had the highest average turnout (63.6 percent) of any three contiguous elections since 1912. To state the matter more clearly: the individually oriented system of electoral participation achieved its greatest success right before a six-election period of uninterrupted decline.

This fact suggests a useful way of gaining insight into the 1960–1980 turnout decline phenomenon. If America in the 1950s represents, in a quantitative sense, the apotheosis of the individual system of voter participation, then the features of this system should be sharply etched in the political history of the period. This should allow the features of the system to be delineated fairly easily by examining the political profile of the era. This, in turn, should provide a basis for deciding which aspects of this system are most likely to have decayed during the 1960s and 1970s, thereby acting to depress turnout levels.

The System of the 1950s

Fortunately, the political profile of Americans in this era was extensively documented through a series of famous studies, including, most prominently, *The American Voter* (1960) and *The Civic Culture* (1963). These studies allow us to draw a fairly detailed portrait of how Americans in the 1950s felt and thought about the political world.

This portrait may be sketched in the following manner (here I draw heavily on the summary of these studies presented in Nie, Verba, and Petrocik 1976, pp. 14–42). First, *the average citizen was involved in political life, but not all that involved.* For most citizens, politics was not central to their everyday concerns. Their concerns focused around jobs, families, health, and other aspects of their personal and daily lives. The only political activity, besides voting, that the majority of the population engaged in was to follow the campaign in the mass media. All other political activities drew the participation of less than 30 percent of the population—28 percent tried to convince someone else to vote for a candidate they liked; 16 percent displayed a campaign button or sticker; only 7 percent attended a political meeting or rally. Thus the chief forms of political involvement, in the system of the 1950s, were the act of voting itself and following election campaigns in the mass media.

Second, *most citizens had strong, long-term commitments to one of the major political parties, and this commitment served as a guide to their political behavior.* Beyond party commitments, the political views of most Americans tended to be inconsistent and unsophisticated. It was really the partisan attachment that defined their relationship to the political world, in general, and to the electoral process, in particular.

Third, *citizens felt relatively satisfied with the political system and relatively efficacious.* That is, not only did most Americans feel that the political system was generally a pretty good one, but they also felt that the ordinary citizen could have a say about what happened within that system. This latter feeling of "efficaciousness"—that citizens could make their voices heard by the powers that be—was quite high in this period, amounting to about two-thirds of the populace.

Finally, *social structurally defined groups of citizens varied widely in their political attitudes and behaviors.* That is, the relationship of Americans to the political world was not uniform across the social structure. Upper-class people did not act and feel the same way as lower-class people; older citizens tended to be different than younger citizens; and so on. This political stratification was particularly noticeable in terms of participation behaviors, including voter turnout.

The sketch of the American electorate drawn by these classic studies suggests some of the ways in which the system of the 1950s worked: (a) Americans involved themselves in election campaigns through individual attention to the media; (b) citizens interpreted election stakes in terms of their individual sense of attachment to the political parties; (c) Americans felt that individual voters would, in some sense, be "heard" by those who wound up running the government after the election; and (d) either these traits (involvement, partisanship, efficaciousness) were not uniformly distributed across the social structure, or there were aspects of social structural position that independently affected the costs and benefits of voting, or both, since different social structural groups found their way to the polls at different rates.

The question now becomes: How might the system of the 1950s have been changed by events in the 1960s and 1970s, such that turnout levels were negatively affected? What changed in American society after 1960 to weaken this (relatively) successful system of individual responsibility for voting?

Two possibilities present themselves. The first is the political traits just described may not have been stable over the 1960–1980 time period. That is, it is plausible that levels of involvement, partisanship, and efficacy among the general population did not remain the same after the 1950s.

For instance, involvement in campaigns could have declined for a couple of reasons. To begin with, it is a common contention that Americans, at least in the 1970s, became generally withdrawn from politics, preferring to concentrate on their personal lives and careers (the "me" decade). Second, recalling that the "involvement" referred to here is pitched at the level of media usage, it is quite possible, given how the role of the mass media in campaigns has changed (increased use of paid media, centrality of television advertising, etc.), that patterns of media usage by citizens have been altered.

It also seems plausible that partisan attachments could have weakened. Again, it is a commonplace that parties mean less to the average citizen than they used to. Indeed, some observers speak of "dealignment" of the electoral system, in which parties have lost their centrality to the political process and have become a relatively weak guide to voting behavior.

Efficacy, too, could easily have declined. A constant theme of popular commentators has been the pervasiveness of "alienation" in American society, of an individual feeling that "I don't matter." Perhaps this feeling has a counterpart in the electoral sphere, eroding that sense of political effectiveness that apparently characterized most Americans in the 1950s.

The second possibility is that the social structure has not been stable over the 1960–1980 time period. That is, it seems plausible that the distribution of individuals among the social structural groups relevant to turnout did not remain the same as it was in the 1950s.

For instance, it has already been mentioned that the distribution of educational attainment changed dramatically between 1960 and 1980 (shifting upward). It seems reasonable to assume that this was not the only demographic change of significance over this time period.

Along these lines, it is generally supposed that American society became younger after 1960, owing to the maturation of the baby boom generation. In addition, of course, there was the constitutional change of 1972 (the Twenty-sixth Amendment) that enfranchised eighteen- to twenty-year-olds, thus specifically making the *voting pool* younger.

It is also generally assumed that, for a variety of reasons, the populace became more mobile and more likely to be single over the 1960–1980 time period. These changes could also be viewed as further significant alterations in the social structure that underpinned the world of *The American Voter*.

Thus a brief consideration of two possible sources of change—political and demographic—suggests reasons why both may have played roles in the weakening of the system of the 1950s. It is now appropriate to take this line of inquiry a step further and flesh out, from a scholarly and substantive standpoint, how and why these sources of change may have figured in post-1960 turnout decline.

Sociopolitical Characteristics

Let us look first at the sociopolitical aspects of change. The three political traits under consideration are involvement, partisanship, and efficacy.

Involvement. It will be recalled that the form of involvement alluded to here is following the election campaign in the mass media. There are three questions to be asked about this type of campaign involvement (which are relevant to all the characteristics to be considered in this section and the next): (1) Does this trait affect turnout? (2) Why does this trait affect turnout? and (3) Is there evidence of distributional change on this trait over the time period in question?

It has been well established in the literature (Prisuta 1973; Reiter 1979; Shaffer 1981) that at least some forms of media involvement correlate positively with turnout (that is, the more involvement, the higher the turnout rate). The form of media involvement that is most strongly and unambiguously correlated with turnout is newspaper reading—following the campaign in the papers.

Why is this so? Why does following an election in the newspapers make a citizen more likely to vote? There are two lines of thought on why this is the case.

According to the first view, the effect of campaign newspaper reading stems from the information absorbed and the active way (relative to television and radio) in which this must be done (Graber 1976; Stevenson 1978). Voters who read the papers not only know more than those who don't, but also are intellectually engaged with what they do know. Elections are therefore more intelligible to them and they vote more often.

The other view locates this characteristic's effect in the level of psychological involvement it either indicates or engenders (or both). People who follow the campaign closely in the papers become involved (or are indicating their involvement) with the election process, and thus have stronger connections to the issues at stake than those who don't. Elections are therefore more meaningful to them and they are more likely to vote.[2]

There is no compelling reason to choose between these two viewpoints. This is because following the campaign closely in the papers should logically be important on both levels. Levels of political understanding *and* psychological involvement should be higher among those who frequently read newspaper articles. And both understanding and psychological involvement should enhance the feelings/commitments that are expressed at the polls, producing the same end result: increased turnout.

The final question is: Did the level of campaign involvement drop between 1960 and 1980? This appears to be the case, as indicated by the data in Table 1-1. In 1960, 55 percent read many articles about the campaign, and only 20 percent read none. By 1980 only 26 percent reported reading many articles, whereas the proportion reading none had climbed to 29 percent.[3] The level of involvement, through the most difficult and demanding of the mass media, therefore dropped substantially over time.

Partisanship. Party identification, as study after study has shown, is strongly related to turnout (Campbell et al. 1960; Verba and Nie 1972; Brody 1978; Cassel and Hill 1981; Shaffer 1981; Abramson and Aldrich 1982). The more partisan toward a political party an individual is, the more likely he or she is to vote. This should come as no surprise, given the well-documented historical role of partisan affiliation and activity in promoting turnout.

The reasons *why* high partisanship facilitates turnout are easy to understand. It makes sense that strong partisan feelings should

Table 1-1
Population Proportions of Turnout-Related Characteristics

	1960	1964	1968	1972	1976	1980
EDUCATION						
0-9 years	.305	.246	.228	.201	.159	.116
9-11	.181	.203	.176	.174	.146	.142
12	.290	.317	.311	.323	.352	.354
13-15	.120	.122	.149	.163	.190	.211
16 or more	.104	.113	.136	.139	.154	.177
AGE						
18-24 years	.033	.072	.079	.148	.143	.145
25-28	.086	.087	.089	.095	.115	.103
29-32	.085	.088	.071	.078	.077	.088
33-36	.103	.076	.070	.061	.076	.088
37 or more	.694	.677	.692	.619	.590	.576
MARITAL STATUS						
not married-SP (1)	.198	.233	.294	.328	.367	.394
married-SP	.802	.767	.706	.672	.633	.606
RESIDENTIAL MOBILITY						
mobile within						
two years	.254	.265	.280*	.296*	.313	.332
not mobile	.746	.735	.720*	.704*	.687	.668
OCCUPATION						
housewives	.249	.306	.283	.266	.222	.160
blue collar (2)	.284	.271	.260	.238	.224	.237
white collar						
and other	.467	.423	.457	.497	.554	.603
FAMILY INCOME						
poor (3)	.434	.364	.356	.339	.381	.347
non-poor	.566	.636	.644	.661	.619	.653
SEX						
female	.542	.557	.563	.573	.588	.563
male	.458	.443	.437	.427	.412	.437
RACE						
non-white	.093	.109	.109	.109	.112	.161
white	.907	.891	.891	.891	.888	.839
REGION						
south	.253	.220	.230	.260	.242	.271
non-south	.747	.780	.770	.740	.758	.729
PARTISANSHIP						
independent,						
apolitical	.126	.090	.116	.133	.159	.147
weak partisan, leaner	.512	.528	.585	.629	.608	.589
strong partisan	.363	.381	.299	.238	.233	.264
POLITICAL EFFICACY						
low efficacy	.153	.206	.334	.294	.353	.319
middle efficacy	.235	.272	.238	.294	.294	.340
high efficacy	.612	.522	.428	.412	.354	.341
CAMPAIGN NEWSPAPER READING						
no articles	.198	.213	.238	.424	.265	.290
some articles	.249	.247	.258	.208	.342	.447
many articles	.553	.540	.504	.369	.393	.263

(1) SP = spouse present
(2) blue collar includes service workers
(3) poor is defined as less than 5000 in 1960 dollars
  * these mobility proportions were interpolated from figures for
    1964 and 1976.

help make individuals care about voting, both by providing an interpretive framework for the issues of a campaign and by making the actual outcome of the election a matter of personal importance. The feelings and commitments expressed by the partisan through voting will thus tend to be clearer and more powerful than for the nonpartisan. Hence the partisan will be more likely to vote.

Turning to the question of distributional change, it is worth noting at the outset that much concerning the relationship of Americans to the political parties changed little over the two decades in question. For instance, the proportion of individuals contacted by parties in the course of a campaign remained stable from 1960 to 1980. Even more interesting, the proportion that saw important differences between the political parties did not decline over the two decades, but went up somewhat. In fact, attempts to show that Americans increasingly view the two parties as identical, from a policy standpoint, have invariably been dismal failures (Wolfinger and Rosenstone 1980). Citizens apparently remain well aware that the Republicans and Democrats stand for significantly different political agendas.

But what has changed is precisely the individual-level sense of identification with the parties that was discussed previously.[4] Partisanship has dropped substantially, as shown in Table 1-1, and as numerous other researchers have noted (Nie, Verba, and Petrocik 1976; Converse 1976). The key change is not so much the rise in pure independents as the sharp decline in strong partisans—well over a third of the electorate in 1960 but only about a quarter in 1980. (Note that the weak partisans are collapsed with independents who lean toward one party. This is because the political behavior of the two groupings is remarkably similar [Nelson et al. 1983].)

Efficacy. Political efficacy (or "external efficacy," as it is frequently termed in the literature) has a long history in the study of voting participation and general electoral behavior. First used in Campbell and colleagues' benchmark study, *The American Voter*, it has since been used in numerous studies of American politics (Verba and Nie 1972; Nie, Verba, and Petrocik 1976; Wright 1976; Shaffer 1981; Abramson and Aldrich 1982). The basic idea of political efficacy is that it taps the extent to which an individual feels that he or she has any power over governmental actions.

The studies cited have all found that the higher an individual's level of political efficacy, the more likely that individual is to vote. This appears to be a consistent and unambiguous relationship. Thus the first question in the set (does this trait affect turnout?) may be answered positively.

The reason why this trait affects turnout may be understood in the following way. First, consider the fact that efficacy is generally measured on the basis of questions that ask a respondent whether people like him or her have any influence on the government (see Appendix for the specific questions on which this concept, when operationalized, is usually based). This means that efficacy, at least as understood in the literature, refers not so much to the idea that citizens, as lone individuals, have power over the government, but to the idea that citizens, grouped in a certain way ("people like me"), have power.

This makes it clearer why efficacy has an effect on turnout. It has already been pointed out that part of the puzzle of voting is that the actions of one individual don't change things, yet people vote. Given this, it doesn't seem surprising that some people need a motivation to overcome the feeling that their vote doesn't matter. For many, this may be provided by the belief (termed by Jon Elster "magical thinking," since no matter *what* people believe, a lone vote *still* doesn't matter) that their individually defined reference group ("people like me") has some power over governmental actions. This allows them to feel that their individual act of voting has significance when considered as a constituent part of a larger process (people like them influencing the government). Conversely, it is easy to see why those who lack this belief would be disinclined to vote. Not only do they, as lone individuals, lack the ability to influence the government, but they also believe that people of their ilk generally lack the power to do so. Such a view would surely make it difficult to see the point in voting.

Turning to the question of distributional change, Table 1-1 indicates that a decline in political efficacy was indeed a factor in the 1960–1980 period. In 1960 the level of political efficacy was actually fairly high—61 percent of the population could be classified as having high efficacy, with only 15 percent having low effi-cacy. This corresponds to the portrait of the 1950s electorate pre-viously discussed. By 1980 this had changed remarkably, with only 34 percent reporting high efficacy and with low efficacy up to 32 percent (Table 1-1; Lipset and Schneider 1983). This is a change of dramatic dimensions, and one not paralleled by other traits, like citizen duty, to which efficacy is sometimes theoretically linked (Abramson and Aldrich 1982).

Summary. Three sociopolitical characteristics have now been identified as of probable salience to declining turnout, and there-fore worth including in the research process. All three character-istics—campaign newspaper reading, partisanship, and political efficacy—appear likely to have contributed directly to the ob-served fall in turnout levels.

The nature of these sociopolitical changes may be conceptual-ized in the following manner. The three basic institutions that link individuals to the electoral process are the political parties, the media, and the state. The political parties actually run the candi-dates and put forward the policies between which citizens must choose. The media are the informational sources through which individuals can follow the progress of a campaign. Finally, the state is the vehicle through which these candidates and policies make their impact on citizens' lives.

Let us recall that the "system of the 1950s" was characterized by fairly strong links between individuals and these institutions. In fact, it was these individual links—individual *commitments* to the political system through belief or behavior—that were crucial in motivating Americans to participate, given the lack of collective supports and collective facilitation of the voting act. Thus it makes sense that if social change of the 1960s and 1970s made individ-uals less inclined to follow politics, less identified with the parties, and less convinced they could influence the government, turnout would fall. They had, in a sense, become disconnected from poli-tics—in some of the only ways that Americans *are* connected to politics—and increasingly lacked the minimal necessary motiva-tion to vote. (And given the nature of the American system, it was unlikely that collectivities, such as the parties or the state, would move to compensate for the attentuation of individual motiva-tion.)

This concept may also be expressed using the traditional descriptive imagery of core and periphery (Tingsten 1937; Campbell et al. 1960). If traits that bind citizens to the electoral system, and thus promote participation, are "core" and those that don't are "peripheral,"[5] then the political periphery would appear to have expanded between 1960 and 1980. A process of political peripheralization may therefore be visualized as a possible key force behind declining turnout.

Social Structural Characteristics

It is now appropriate to turn to the possible role that social structural change may have played in undermining the system of the 1950s and contributing to the fall in voter participation. As with the sociopolitical traits, I will deal with three questions about each trait: (1) Does the trait affect turnout? (2) Why does it affect turnout? and (3) Did the distribution on this trait change much over time? The first characteristics discussed will be education, occupation, and income—the three components of socioeconomic status (SES).

Socioeconomic Status. SES has repeatedly been shown to affect turnout (Campbell et al. 1960; Verba and Nie 1972; Lipset 1981). These effects may be summarized in the following manner: (a) the higher the level of educational attainment, the more likely a person is to vote; (b) the less manual the occupation, the more likely a person is to vote; and (c) the higher the level of income, the more likely the person is to vote. The reasons why SES has these effects on turnout are usually attributed, in the literature, to its role as a "facilitator" of voter participation.

Education, for instance, increases cognitive skills, which are viewed as making it easier to learn about a complex and abstract subject like politics. It also increases the ability to handle bureaucratic obstacles such as those entailed by registration (Wolfinger and Rosenstone 1980). Nonmanual occupations are believed to provide more mental stimulation, access to information, and opportunity for insight into complex social mechanisms (Lipset 1981). And a higher income is said to allow the voter to "lift his head" from the preoccupations of daily life and take the time and emotional energy necessary for a nonessential like voting (as well as perhaps increasing his or her stake in the system, and thus, presumably, the stake in the election outcome).

These effects may be summed up by saying that higher SES is believed to make it *easier* for a citizen to vote, by increasing his or her ability to deal with the mechanics (informational, cognitive, bureaucratic) of the voting process. Although these assertions are difficult, if not impossible, to prove, owing to the intrinsic nature of the relationship between social structural background characteristics and a cognitively oriented behavior like voting, they will be accepted here because of their basic plausibility and consensual validity.

We can now examine the question of distributional change on these characteristics. First, as mentioned earlier, one component of SES, education, is widely known to have trended up—dramatically in fact—rather than down, during this period. Further, the real income distribution also shifted upward over the two decades (Thurow 1981, pp. 41–75). Finally, occupational shifts reduced the proportions of blue-collar workers and housewives, two groups less likely to vote, according to the logic outlined previously (data on distributional change for all three SES components may be found in Table 1-1).

Thus the 1960–1980 period was characterized by a general pattern of socioeconomic *upgrading*, which all other things being equal, should have facilitated voter participation. In other words, not just education went up, but also income and occupation. This underscores the nature of the "puzzle," alluded to at the beginning of this analysis, that key social developments trended in a direction that was *inconsistent* with the observed fall in voter participation.

Socioeconomic variables are, for precisely this reason, quite salient to the topic under investigation and cannot be ignored in the analysis. On the contrary, they are a crucial part of that analysis.[6] This can be understood in two ways. First, it is possible that the effects of SES on turnout changed so drastically over the time period that the net impact on turnout levels, despite the distributional upgrading, was zero or negative. This possibility should be checked, since it would help explain why turnout went down, not up, over the two decades.

Second—and far more important—if the scenario corresponding to the first possibility did not occur (which seems likely), this would mean that turnout levels actually did receive an upward "push" from socioeconomic upgrading. In turn, this would imply that the upward push on turnout from the upgrading must somehow have been countered by downward pressure from other sources that were strong enough to (a) "cancel out" this upward push and (b) bring turnout down to the levels observed in the real world. In this sense, the effects of socioeconomic upgrading would then constitute an "extra" amount of turnout decline to be explained, and thus an integral part of the problem to be solved (again, exactly why the problem can properly be termed a "puzzle").

Age, Residential Mobility, and Marital Status. These variables have also been shown, time and again, to affect turnout (Campbell et al. 1960; Wolfinger and Rosenstone 1980; Lipset 1981; Cassel and Hill 1981; Shaffer 1981). Their effects can be described as follows: (a) older members of the electorate vote more frequently than their younger counterparts; (b) individuals with stable residences vote more frequently than those who have been recently mobile; and (c) individuals who are married and living with their spouses vote more frequently than those who are single.

The reason why these characteristics affect turnout is generally attributed to the relationship between them and how "rooted" the individual is within the social structure and political system. That is, these traits are associated with personal ties and experiences that, on balance, help the voters absorb the costs of, and derive the necessary motivation for, casting a ballot.

Growing older, for instance, increases a citizen's experience with the voting process, both in dealing with the bureaucratic requirements of voting and in making sense of the political information necessary to distinguish between candidates. Those who have not been recently mobile have the advantages of established ties within their immediate political environment, as well as not having to deal with basic start-up costs of relocation, including, of course, re-registration. Finally, those who are married and living with their spouses can share the physical costs of voting (like registering and traveling to the polling booth), as well as the task of deciding between candidates. In addition, those who are "settled down" may feel more of a stake in an election's outcome because of concerns relating to children, community, and so on.

Again, it is difficult to say with complete assurance that these explanations are the "correct" ones, but they will be accepted here nonetheless. Their plausibility and consensual status within the literature make them satisfactory for the purposes of this investigation.

Turning now to the question of distributional changes, it may easily be seen from the data presented in Table 1-1 that such changes were quite significant during the 1960–1980 period. To begin with, it is clear that the voting pool did become younger over these two decades. Part of this, of course, was due to the enfranchisement of eighteen- to twenty-year-olds, alluded to previously, but the age distribution of the population was shifting toward the younger end of the spectrum even before 1972. And the electorate certainly became more residentially mobile and less traditional in their marital/living arrangements. In 1960, for example, 75 percent of the population had not moved within two years, whereas in 1980 this proportion had decreased to 67 percent. More impressive, in 1960, 80 percent of the electorate were married and living with their spouses, whereas by 1980 this figure had fallen to only 61 percent.[7] Thus a substantial decline of the "rootedness" of individuals within the social structure appears to have been a factor within this period. And in contrast to socioeconomic change, this set of changes—in the age, mobility, and marital status distributions— trends in a direction consistent with the observed fall in turnout.

Race, Region, and Sex. These attributes have all been shown, at one time or another, to have effects on turnout (Campbell et al. 1960; Reiter 1979; Wolfinger and Rosenstone 1980; Lipset 1981). These findings, however, are considerably less uniform and unambiguous than those applicable to the other social structural characteristics in this section. With this caveat in mind, the effects of these characteristics on turnout are generally described in the following manner: (a) whites are more likely to vote than nonwhites; (b) those outside the South are more likely to vote than those in it; and (c) men are more likely to vote than women.

The explanation for these effects is usually located in the nature of the divisions captured by these attributes. That is, these divisions—white/nonwhite, South/non-South, men/women—are seen as divisions between those more "outside" than "inside" the electoral system, owing to socialization, culture, legal obstacles, general way of life, and other factors (Key 1949; Campbell et al. 1960;

Lipset 1981). For those inside the system, voting is said to be easier, since there are fewer "barriers" to participation for them to contend with. Thus men, whites, and non-Southerners vote at higher rates.

As noted in previous cases, these theoretical contentions are, by the nature of their subject matter, not really susceptible to "proof." For this reason they should be treated with a certain amount of caution. Still they seem plausible as explanations for why such characteristics would have effects independent of other social structural attributes. Given this, and their consensual status within the literature, they will be treated as adequate for the purposes of this analysis.

Turning to the question of distributional change, there does not seem to have been much of a change in the distribution of the population into racial, sexual, and regional categories over the time period. However, there does appear to be a real possibility that the effects of these characteristics on turnout changed over the two decades. This is because the relative situations of men and women, blacks and whites, Southerners and non-Southerners are believed to have altered between 1960 and 1980. However these changes are assessed, it is generally agreed that these groups became more equal to one another in important respects. This may have reduced the extent to which racial, sexual, and regional divisions posed barriers to participation, and thereby changed the effects of these characteristics on turnout.

The possibility just described receives some support from the work of Reiter (1979) and Santi (1982). They describe a decline in the effects of these characteristics that is reflected in the narrowing of differences in aggregate turnout rates by race, region, and sex. These changes are believed to have played a role in declining turnout.[8]

There is an important problem with this view. That is, it is not clear to what extent these characteristics really do have an effect on turnout, once other social structural characteristics are controlled for (Wolfinger and Rosenstone 1980, pp. 41–44, 90–94). For all three of these variables, but particularly for race and sex, there are strong differences along socioeconomic distributional lines that account for much of the variation among categories. Given this, it could also be true that changes in aggregate voting rate differentials between whites and nonwhites, men and women, Southerners and non-Southerners could simply reflect the different ways in which socioeconomic trends have affected these groups. Neither of the investigators mentioned earlier considers this possibility.

This means that although it is worthwhile to investigate the possibility that the effects of these characteristics have changed, this should only be done while controlling for other social structural characteristics. In such a context, it can be determined, first, whether race, region, and sex have independent effects on turnout and, then, whether these effects have changed over time.

Summary. Nine social structural characteristics have now been identified as of possible relevance to turnout decline. Of the nine, three—the SES variables, education, occupation, and income—appear likely to have been countervailing forces to the observed fall in voter participation. Three others, age, residential mobility, and marital status, may have contributed directly to declining turnout. With the final three, race, region, and sex, it is unclear whether any—and what kinds of—effects on turnout levels are likely to have occurred.

The probable overall role of social structure in turnout decline is thus difficult to assess. There are, in fact, three possibilities that present themselves: (1) the net impact of social structural change on turnout levels may turn out to be positive because of the strong effects of socioeconomic upgrading; (2) the overall role of these characteristics may be zero because all factors cancel out; and (3) the net impact of demographic change may account for all or part of the decline in turnout, if the contributions from the non-SES factors are strong enough to overcome the effects of socioeconomic upgrading.

Put a little more concretely, social change in the 1960s and 1970s can be viewed as having made America more of a "middle class" society, most particularly in terms of educational attainment. Given the theoretical views presented here, and certainly by the canons of 1950s social science, this should have made America more of a participatory society. On the other side of the ledger, members of the electorate became, on the whole, less rooted in the social structure, probably discouraging participation, by these same theories and canons. And then there is the unpredictable influence of the trends toward racial, regional, and sexual equality.

What was the resultant of all these forces? This is really the question. Did this array of social structural changes, in the aggregate, make it easier for the U.S. electorate to participate, have no effect, or make it harder? Expressed another way, drawing on the core-periphery imagery previously introduced (core traits facilitating access to the system, peripheral ones making such access more difficult), did the demographic core of the electorate expand, stay the same, or contract?

This imagery, in fact, may be extended to the general nature of the research project under consideration. The following possibilities have been suggested by the analyses and trends presented in the previous two sections: (a) the demographic core expanded, but political peripheralization was strong enough to both compensate for that upward "push" *and* bring turnout down to observed levels; (b) the demographic core did not change in size, and the expansion of the political periphery was largely responsible for the fall in turnout; and (c) the demographic periphery *and* political periphery expanded, thus jointly causing the decline in turnout levels. Which of these is the true story, or whether none of them are, is the question to be adjudicated through the research process.

Empirical Studies of Turnout Decline

Before a strategy for the research process is elaborated, however, it is worthwhile to review previous studies that have attempted to solve the "puzzle" of turnout decline. This will allow the strategy to be informed by the methodology and results of these earlier studies.

Although much has been written on the general subject of falling turnout, there have been surprisingly few empirical analyses devoted to the problem. Of these, a number do not purport to have solved the puzzle, but rather to have located factors that played a role in turnout decline. Cavanaugh (1981) and Boyd (1981) have targeted increasing youthfulness of the electorate as an important influence. Similarly, Brody (1978) and Cassel and Hill (1981) claim that declining partisanship is of salience, while decreased political efficacy is mentioned by Campbell (1979) and Clotfelter and Prysby (1980). All of this is consistent with my own discussion of factors likely to be relevant to turnout decline.

There are actually only two empirical studies that claim to have substantially solved the turnout decline puzzle. These studies, by Shaffer (1981) and Abramson and Aldrich (1982), each conclude that the factors used in their analyses can account for two-thirds or more of the fall in participation since 1960. They are both excellent studies but have key flaws that render their findings less compelling than claimed.

One of these, the Abramson and Aldrich piece, will be considered in particular detail for several reasons: (1) their study is methodologically elegant and provides much useful guidance in this respect; (2) they cover the same time period as this investigation (1960–1980), whereas Shaffer's analysis goes only through 1976; and (3) their work is the focus of an ongoing debate about turnout decline being conducted in the pages of the *American Political Science Review* (Cassel and Hill 1983). The study, which estimates the effect of two characteristics, partisanship and political efficacy, on falling voter participation, is discussed below.

The data set they use is derived from the American National Election Studies (ANES) and pools all white respondents in the preelection/postelection samples from the six presidential elections in this time period (1960, 1964, 1968, 1972, 1976, and 1980). The statistical methodology used is a form of regression analysis that uses the probit model as its basis (probit analysis is discussed at length in chapter 2). Using the pooled data set, they estimated a series of probit models that linked turnout to partisanship, political efficacy, or both.

These models deserve to be commented on in more detail. For each characteristic, and for both considered together, the authors estimated three models. Using partisanship as an example, they first ran a model that linked this characteristic alone to turnout. This model is represented in equation form as follows:

$$y = a + bp \qquad (1)$$

(Note here that y represents the predicted probit, not probability of voting. This is explained in detail in chapter 2.) They then added terms to estimate the effect of time on turnout, once partisanship had been controlled for. This entailed using five dummy variables, one each for 1964, 1968, 1972, 1976, and 1980 (1960 was used as the reference category). This model is represented as

$$y = a_{60} + bp + c_i t_i \quad (i = 64, 68, 72, 76, 80) \quad (2)$$

Finally, they ran a model that included partisanship, the time dummies, and interaction terms between partisanship and each time dummy, so that changes in the effect of partisanship over time could be examined. This is summarized in equation form as

$$y = a_{60} + b_{60}p + c_i t_i + b_i p t_i \quad (i = 64, 68, 72, 76, 80) \quad (3)$$

The extensions to the case of political efficacy alone, and to partisanship and efficacy considered together, are obvious.

The authors conclude, using a model of the form of Equation 1, which includes both characteristics, that distributional decreases in partisanship and political efficacy explain about two-thirds of the drop in turnout between 1960 and 1980. They reach this conclusion by generating the predicted level of turnout for 1960 (done by substituting the 1960 means for partisanship and efficacy into the equation) and then comparing it with that predicted for 1980 (using the 1980 means). The difference between the 1960 and 1980 figures represents the amount of turnout decline predicted by the model. This quantity may then be compared with the amount of turnout decline reported in the data set. The ratio between the predicted and reported amounts is the proportion of turnout decline accounted for by the model—in this case, two-thirds.

This study may be criticized on several grounds. The first problem concerns the construction of the authors' data set. As mentioned earlier, they confine this data set to white respondents in the ANES surveys. Their rationale for this is that trends among the white and the black subpopulations are different with respect to both the dependent variable (turnout) and one of the independent variables (partisanship). (An analogous rationale is used by Shaffer [1981] to exclude respondents in the South from his analysis.) This does not seem like an adequate reason for ignoring an important subpopulation. It is possible, for instance, that the reason why turnout trends are in the opposite direction for blacks is precisely because the trend for partisanship is also in the opposite direction, a development that would be entirely consistent with the simple model they estimate. In any event, since they are ostensibly investigating turnout decline in America (not *white* America), it would be preferable to put in a dummy variable for race rather than exclude the subpopulation. This is especially desirable because there are substantive reasons for believing that the effects of race (and region) may have changed over the 1960–1980 time period.

The second problem is more serious than the previous one, since it casts immediate doubt on the extent to which their model accounts for turnout decline. This concerns the omission of education, occupation, and income from their model. I will focus my discussion here on the omission of education, since (a) Abramson and Aldrich do directly address their exclusion of this variable, although they do not mention occupation or income, and (b) the problem posed by ignoring education is much the sharpest of the three variables.

The rationale given for their procedure is that increased educational attainment acted to retard the decline in turnout, and hence need not be considered. The first part of their statement is indeed true. The changing educational distribution, as discussed earlier, did almost certainly act to push turnout up—that is, as a countervailing force to the overall downward trend. But it does not follow that therefore the effect of education can be ignored.

This may be understood by recalling why the decline in turnout has been termed a "puzzle" in the literature. One of the main reasons (if not *the* main reason) cited has been the fact that the educational distribution trended in a direction inconsistent with the observed fall in voter participation. Thus, by eliminating education from their analysis, they actually define away a good deal of what makes the problem they are looking at a puzzle. This is not acceptable. Investigation of turnout decline in this period should take into account the fact that, exactly because of the increase in educational attainment, there is a sharper decrease in turnout to be explained than would be assumed from simply looking at reported turnout levels.

This is the same general point made by Cassel and Hill (1983) in a communication to the *American Political Science Review* concerning Abramson and Aldrich's article. They observe: "Why did turnout decline when factors such as increased education of the electorate should have engendered an increase in voting? . . . We cannot help but wonder how much of the explanatory power of the author's two-variable model would evaporate if the offsetting power of education was introduced into the model" (p. 1011). In their own (1981) article on the same subject, Cassel and Hill included education in their model (as well as partisanship, efficacy, and other variables) and found that, partly because of the "offsetting" effect of schooling, they could account for only a small proportion of the fall in voter participation. This underscores the relevance of including education in any model purporting to explain turnout decline. Without it, a model will always be open to the criticism that, if education should be included, the results in question would look more like Cassel and Hill's than like Abramson and Aldrich's. Clearly, then, an adequate study will substantially account for turnout decline, even in the presence of the countervailing force of increased educational attainment (and socioeconomic upgrading, in general).

There is one rationale for excluding education that, if well founded, could adequately justify this exclusion. This is the claim that all of education's effect on turnout is through intervening attitudinal/behavioral variables.[9] By this view, education is strictly an antecedent variable in the determination of turnout, and therefore need not be considered. There is, however, not a shred of empirical evidence that this is true. Nor is it claimed anywhere in the literature that the effect of education can be theoretically interpreted in this way, including by Abramson and Aldrich themselves. Education must therefore still be considered relevant to analyzing turnout decline.

The third problem is really an expanded version of the one just alluded to. That is, Abramson and Aldrich's model is indeed pleasingly parsimonious, being limited to only two variables, but is that parsimony justified? Their own justification is that they need only consider voter characteristics that (a) have a demonstrated, independent relationship to turnout and (b) have significantly changed in the aggregate over the time period.

The first point is difficult to argue with. If a given characteristic bears no relationship to turnout, it is reasonable to assume that that characteristic has no relationship to turnout decline. The second point is also reasonable, but there is one qualification that should be made. That is, it is not true that a characteristic needs to have changed distributionally to figure in turnout decline. It is possible that the effect of a variable may have changed in such a way that, despite the distribution on that variable remaining exactly the same, the impact on turnout will be in a downward direction. This possibility was discussed earlier, when the role of race, region, and sex in turnout decline was considered. However, because they implicitly recognize this by fitting a model allowing the effects of partisanship and efficacy to vary over time, and the results do not suggest that this possibility is relevant here, their two points may be accepted in context.

The real problem is that even by their own criteria of turnout-related characteristics that have changed in the aggregate, Abramson and Aldrich are inconsistent. First, by "changed in the aggregate" they really mean "changed in the aggregate in such a way as to contribute to turnout decline." Hence their exclusion of a variable like education. This is unacceptable for the reasons discussed previously.

Second, and even more damaging, they ignore a number of turnout-related characteristics that not only changed distributionally, but also changed in a way consistent with the fall in voter participation (presumably exactly what they were looking for). These characteristics have all been mentioned in previous discussion and will be reviewed here only briefly.

First, the 1960–1980 time period witnessed an expansion of the younger segment of the electorate (maturation of the baby boom generation, enfranchisement of eighteen-year-olds). Most strikingly, the proportion under age twenty-five increased from 3 percent in 1960 to 15 percent in 1980. Second, there was a substantial increase in residential mobility, going from 25 percent in 1960 to 33 percent in 1980. Third, there was a sharp increase in the proportion of those not living as married couples (from 20 percent to 39 percent). Finally, there was a strong decrease in the extent to which people followed the campaign in the newspapers. The proportion paying close attention to the campaign in the papers—

reading many articles—went from 55 percent in 1960 to 26 percent in 1980.

Abramson and Aldrich, however, do not even mention any of these variables, if only to explain why they are not using them. Besides the general problems of inconsistency and incompleteness that this raises, there is a particular problem, within the framework of their research findings, that is highlighted by a diagram in their own article.

This diagram plots turnout levels predicted by their model (the one with partisanship and efficacy, in the form of equation [1]), as well as turnout levels reported in the ANES data. The graph shows that the model predicts turnout decline very well from 1960 through 1968, but after 1968 it does a considerably poorer job, substantially underpredicting the extent of the decline. The fact that the usefulness of their model drastically decreases after 1968 should have told them that probably factors were left out of their model that were depressing turnout during these years. In addition, the fact that the coefficients of the time dummies in their second model (equation [2]) were all significant from 1972 on should have told them the same thing.

The characteristics just described—those that satisfied their own criteria but were omitted from the model—shed considerable light on this problem. First, it may be recalled that the increased youthfulness of the electorate had its strongest impact after 1968 because of the enfranchisement of eighteen- to twenty-year-olds. Second, the decline in campaign newspaper reading is really concentrated in the post-1968 era. This may be seen by looking at Table 1-1. For instance, between 1960 and 1968 the proportion reading many articles about the campaign declined only 5 percent, from 55 percent to 50 percent. But between 1968 and 1972 this proportion dropped to 37 percent and by 1980 had dipped to 26 percent. Clearly the overwhelming amount of this change occurs after 1968, precisely the years in which Abramson and Aldrich's model ceases to fit well. These observations illustrate the practical implications of leaving out relevant characteristics and suggest the potential usefulness of such characteristics in an analysis of turnout decline.

These criticisms of the Abramson and Aldrich article are all applicable, in one degree or another, to the study by Shaffer (1981).

He, too, unnecessarily restricts his population, in this case, by excluding Southerners and those under age twenty-one. He also ignores the increase in educational attainment, even though, by his own calculations, its effect on turnout levels is fully a third in magnitude of all the other factors in his model. And finally, although he does include age and campaign newspaper reading in his analysis, he excludes residential mobility and marital status. Thus his study, although more complete in certain respects than the one just described, suffers from the same basic flaws.

This concludes the review of empirical studies concerning the fall in voter participation. The following lessons for this inquiry into the topic are suggested: (a) the data set should include all subpopulations of the eligible electorate; (b) the role of increased educational attainment, in particular, and socioeconomic upgrading, in general, in retarding turnout decline should not be ignored, but considered an integral part of the puzzle to be solved; (c) characteristics besides partisanship and political efficacy should be examined. These characteristics should include, at a minimum, education, age, residential mobility, marital status, and campaign newspaper reading; and (d) an attempt should be made to periodize turnout decline, since it appears that different factors may have been particularly influential in different periods. These points are all consistent with the general analysis of turnout and possible influences on turnout decline that was presented earlier in the chapter.

It is now appropriate to turn to the formulation of a specific analytical strategy to study turnout decline.

Notes

1. This is an example of the classic "free rider" problem discussed by Olson (1957), with the outcome of the election as the "public good."

2. One other possibility is that campaign newspaper reading is simply an indicator of campaign interest, and that, therefore, the relationship of newspaper reading to turnout is simply an expression of the relationship between interest and participation. This does not turn out to be the case. Interest attenuates the effect of newspaper reading on turnout, but only moderately.

3. Other forms of campaign media usage did not substantially decline over this time period. Television usage, for instance, which might have been expected to drop in tandem with newspaper reading, actually went up slightly (although not enough to suggest that people were switching their campaign media preference from newspapers to television).

4. The proportion of citizens who "cared a good deal" which party won the election also declined quite a bit over this period (based on responses to this item on the American National Election Studies survey). This characteristic, though, is highly correlated with party identification, so that the two variables together account for little more variation in turnout, and turnout levels, than partisanship alone. Moreover, it is likely, based on both theoretical plausibility and empirical evidence, that the decline in this "concern" characteristic is, itself, primarily a reflection of the decline in partisanship (Rollenhagen 1981, cited in Abramson and Aldrich 1982). For these reasons I chose to include only partisanship in my analysis.

5. Core and periphery are not meant in the sense of two mutually exclusive groups, to which all citizens are assigned. Rather, it should be thought of as a sort of probability gradient, on which individuals are located by (a) their set of demographic traits and (b) the relative weights of the effects that social structural characteristics have on turnout.

6. Socioeconomic variables can easily be operationalized and their impact measured, in contrast to changing registration requirements, another possible upward push on turnout. This is because registration reform (a) did not take place on the individual level and (b) had an impact on registration statutes across the United States. An additional factor is that many states have few respondents in a survey like that of the American National Election Studies (only 1,500 respondents nationwide), making a state-by-state breakdown of registration requirements impossible.

7. It is possible that some of the change may be attributable to an increased proportion of people cohabitating. If true, this would be of theoretical salience, given that much of the effect of being married and living with a spouse is attributed to the presence of a partner. Unfortunately, the data does not allow this possibility to be taken into account, since "cohabs" are not measured in either the earlier or the later surveys. The impact of this measurement difficulty may be indirectly checked, however, by seeing if the effect of marital status on turnout changes over time. An attentuation of the effect would be some indication that the problem exists.

8. Whether this role served to promote or depress turnout, however, cannot be deduced from establishing that a change in effect occurred. If, for instance, blacks became more like whites, this would be a factor in-

creasing turnout, whereas if it were the other way around, it would decrease participation.

9. Even if this is true, however, it still means that increased educational attainment would have pushed up turnout, but through a set of intervening variables, rather than "on its own." The puzzle would remain, then, but in a different form.

2

Framing the Investigation: Analytical Strategy and Statistical Methods

Analytical Strategy

The strategy elaborated here is a general plan that breaks down the study of turnout decline into a sequence of feasible research tasks. The point here is not to go over every step that will be taken in the investigation (these steps are discussed in detail in the appropriate chapters) or to delve deeply into questions of data or statistical method (these are covered in other sections of the book), but to outline the basic logic that will guide the research process.

This logic should start with one basic fact: there is more turnout decline to be accounted for than would be obvious from simply looking at trends in reported turnout. This observation is derived from discussion about the relationship between turnout levels and socioeconomic upgrading. Because the effect of upgrading should have been to push up turnout levels, the forces pushing down these levels decreased turnout not only by the amount reported in the population, but also by the amount necessary to counteract this upward push. The reported turnout levels do not capture this extra amount of turnout decline and, in this sense, underestimate the magnitude of the drop in turnout to be explained. In contrast to previous investigators, then, I will start by estimating the effect of socioeconomic upgrading on turnout levels. This "socioeconomic (SES)-adjusted" decline will be the real target of the investigation.

The next step is to locate the factors to which the SES-adjusted decrease can be attributed. This task may be descriptively summarized by referring to Table 2-1, which shows the logical possibilities that should be investigated. The diagram is a fourfold table that typologizes influences on turnout decline. The table crosses the two kinds of factors, demographic and sociopolitical, with the two kinds of change through which they may affect turnout levels, distribution and effect. The idea here is that any given factor may contribute to decreased voter participation through aggregate change in the characteristic, change in its effect on turnout, or both. The table reflects this range of possibilities.

The first row of the table—cells 1 and 2, that tap the role of demographic characteristics in turnout decline—will be examined first. These characteristics are education, occupation, income, age, residential mobility, marital status, race, region, and sex. Beginning the investigation this way will allow the effect of socioeconomic upgrading to be examined in the context of other social structural changes. Specifically, we shall see to what extent these other changes can (a) compensate for the upward push from SES upgrading, and (b) if the effect of upgrading can be accounted for, explain the rest of the fall in turnout. This will allow us to determine whether changes in the background characteristics of the electorate have, on balance, made participation easier, had no effect, or made it harder.

Once this determination is made, it will be appropriate to intro-

Table 2-1
Typology of Explanations for Turnout Decline

	distribution	effect
social structural characteristics	1	2
socio-political characteristics	3	4

duce sociopolitical variables into the analysis—factors that tap the relationship of individuals to the political system. These factors were selected on the basis that they (a) are strongly related to turnout and (b) underwent serious distributional change in the 1960–1980 time period. The variables that met this criteria are partisanship, political efficacy, and campaign newspaper reading. Once the impact of these three factors has been assessed, a decision can be made about whether to introduce other characteristics into the investigation. If the SES-adjusted decline in turnout has essentially been explained, this phase of the research process can be brought to a halt and responsibility for the fall in turnout allotted among all the factors—demographic and sociopolitical—that have been included in the model. If a substantial part of turnout decline remains unaccounted for, other characteristics can be introduced into the analysis, to see whether they may explain the remainder of the fall in participation.

This procedure should account for turnout decline to the extent it is possible to do so, given limitations of data and method. The implicit reference point for the above discussion, however, has been the turnout differential between 1960 and 1980, the two end points of the time period in question. This parallels the approach of previous researchers and is indeed a valid focus for the bulk of the investigation. Explaining this differential, though, does not tell the whole of the turnout decline story and, in this sense, does not entirely solve the "puzzle" that constitutes the agenda of this research effort.

There are, in fact, at least two additional aspects of the story that will merit attention at this point in the investigation. The first involves looking at other turnout differentials besides that between 1960 and 1980. This is motivated by (a) empirical evidence that different factors were particularly influential at different times; and (b) the theoretical improbability that the relative weights of the various demographic and sociopolitical factors were constant over the two-decade time span, since historical change typically works in an uneven fashion. Analyzing other differentials, besides the 1960–1980 one, will allow the changing relative weights of different factors to be assessed. The next step in the analysis, therefore, will be to periodize the process of turnout decline, so that this part of the story can be effectively told.

This periodization, however performed, will raise the second additional aspect of the puzzle to be dealt with. Assuming that some of the sociopolitical factors described previously are found to be more influential in certain parts of the 1960–1980 time period than in others, it will be logical to ask why this is so. To what more basic changes can the observed patterns of sociopolitical change be attributed? There may be a number of plausible explanations at that point in the investigation, ranging from the sequencing of historical events to underlying structural change. An attempt to adjudicate between such explanations will therefore be made, so that the story of falling voter participation can be fleshed out in this respect.

The analytical strategy has now been described in enough detail to proceed with the investigation. But before the strategy can be implemented, it is necessary to describe the statistical methods with which the research will be pursued.

This discussion deals with (a) the fact that data must be analyzed from six points in time (1960, 1964, 1968, 1972, 1976, and 1980); (b) the statistical technique used to model individual-level turnout; and (c) how to build models using this technique that will provide insight into the question of turnout decline.

Statistical Methods

Pooling the Data. As is common in research of this nature, the time structure of the data will be dealt with by pooling the individual surveys—six in this case—into one large data set. A variable will then be created to code the year in which the respondent was interviewed.

There are two advantages to doing this. First, it enables the effects of time to be examined directly as the data is analyzed. This is desirable, since the aim of the research project is essentially to see if the time trend in turnout can be explained through the influence of variables other than time. In other words, the most felicitous outcome of the investigation would be to eliminate the effect of time on predicting turnout. This, of course, cannot be done unless time can be included as a variable in the models under consideration.

The second advantage is that parameter estimates can be based on a much larger number of cases (about six times as many), hence considerably enhancing their reliability. Admittedly, it could be objected that the nature of the respondents in some years may be substantially different than it is in others, thereby making the estimates based on the pooled data severely biased. Given, however, that the American National Election Studies (ANES) samples are independent, probability samples of the entire U.S. population for each of the years in question, there appears to be no compelling theoretical reason to sustain this objection. In fact, the only way in which the samples should systematically differ is that they were taken at different points of time. This, of course, will be controlled for by the addition of the time variable to the data set and the determination, through statistical tests (discussed in the next section), of whether differences over time in the effects of variables exist. For all these reasons, therefore, pooling the data in the research process seems a legitimate and useful procedure.

Modeling Individual-level Turnout. It is now appropriate to ask how the relationship between turnout and individual characteristics is to be modeled. This is, at root, a theoretical question, having to do with how one believes such characteristics affect an individual's probability of voting. In other words, what is the general shape of the curve that plots the relationship between the probability of voting (the dependent variable) and the values of the variables that tap individual characteristics (the independent variables)?

The first possibility is a straight line going through the origin. The idea here is simple and corresponds to the kind of curve that would be generated were ordinary least squares (OLS) regression used to model this relationship. A unit increase on the independent variable (IV) generates a uniform increase on the dependent variable (DV) equal to the regression coefficient of the IV in question, no matter where on the curve the individual is located.

There are two things wrong with this. The first is that, because of the nature of the OLS procedure, values outside the 0-1 interval can be generated for the DV. But since the DV here is the probability of voting, this is clearly an undesirable property. Predicted probabilities greater than one or less than zero are meaningless, and hence should be avoided in the modeling procedure.

The second problem is that the increases in probability are uniform, regardless of location on the curve. This is equivalent to assuming that the effect of a particular variable is the same for all types of people. This is probably not a warranted assumption. Although the benefits, costs, and resources pertinent to voting undoubtedly accumulate, they may do so in a nonadditive way. If so, their marginal effect on the probability of voting is not likely to be constant across individuals. One way this might work is the following.

For people almost certain not to vote, the marginal effect of a variable will be small. That is, those for whom the costs of voting seem high and the benefits low will be relatively unaffected by a marginal change in costs or benefits. The task of voting will still seem arduous and pointless. But as the balance between costs and benefits becomes more equal, it will take less to tip the individual in the direction of voting.

A second threshold is reached when the individual is 50 percent likely to vote. After this point the effect of marginal changes in costs and benefits will begin to decrease. This continues until the individuals who are almost certain to vote are reached. As with those almost certain not to vote, the marginal effect of characteristics will be small. An individual for whom the benefits of voting are already high and the costs low is not likely to be much more inclined to vote by making the benefits somewhat higher.

This means that, for example, the college-educated, high-income professional who reads the paper everyday and feels highly efficacious will not derive much additional motivation from a high level of partisanship. For the working-class, middle-income voter with a high school education who seldom reads the paper and feels only somewhat efficacious, the same high level of partisanship may be the crucial motivation for going to the polls. This seems more reasonable than assuming that both voters would be equally affected by their level of partisanship.

Thus the OLS curve both generates uninterpretable predictions and generates predictions in a manner that probably does not correspond to the real world. A curve that corrects these problems is an S-shaped curve, where the predicted probability asymptotically approaches 1, as the value of the IV goes to + infinity, and asymptotically approaches 0, as the IV's value goes to − infinity. This means, of course, that the predicted probability never goes under 0 or over 1, no matter what values are assumed by the IV.

And as is obvious from the shape of the curve, the effect of the IV on the likelihood of voting varies, depending on the location on the curve.

This S-shaped curve, then, has the properties (a) of never predicting probabilities of voting less than 0 or greater than 1 and (b) of describing a functional relationship between voting probabilities and individual characteristics that seems theoretically and practically plausible. Both of these properties are in direct contrast with the undesirable OLS properties outlined previously. This suggests that the S-shaped curve is an appropriate model for analyzing the relationship between turnout and various sociopolitical and demographic traits.

The question now becomes: What form of statistical analysis can be used to model this relationship in the desired fashion? There are basically two choices: probit analysis and logit analysis. These are the two methodologies that are typically used by social scientists and others when analyzing a discrete dependent variable, as I am doing (see Hannushek and Jackson 1977, pp. 179–216, for a clear and thorough discussion of both forms of analysis). In terms of the shape of the curve that links the DV with the IVs, there is little difference between probit and logit, with the probit function approaching 0 and 1 probabilities just a little bit faster than the logit function.

In this analysis the probit model has been chosen. This is not because probit has any advantages, technically speaking, over logit for this investigation. On the contrary, the results produced by either method, in substantive terms, are likely to be virtually identical (Hannushek and Jackson 1977; Mare 1983). The reason why probit is used is simply because it has been used in previous studies of turnout (Wolfinger and Rosenstone 1980; Abramson and Aldrich 1982), whereas logit has not. The use of probit will therefore promote ease of comparison with earlier analyses, as well as the accessibility of this particular study to other researchers on the subject.

It is worthwhile, before proceeding further, to describe the probit model in more detail. The first thing that must be understood about this model (and the key difference between it and OLS regression) is that the prediction derived from the IVs is not of the DV itself (i.e., a probability), but rather of a "probit." What this probit really represents is the distance from 0 in a standard normal distribution. This number is then transformed into a probability by taking the area under the curve up to that distance from the origin (i.e., from − infinity to that point on the x-axis). This area under the curve may range from 0 to 1 and is simply the value of the cumulative standard normal distribution for the probit value under consideration. This is why the cumulative standard normal distribution is referred to as the "link function," since it links the predicted probit—in theory, the *linear part* of the DV—to the DV itself (here the probability of voting). Further, the existence and nature of this link function make it clear why predictions directly based on the values of the IVs may range from − infinity to + infinity, just as in OLS, but the predicted *probabilities* will range only from 0 to 1 (see Baker and Nelder 1978 for a more extensive and technical exposition of link functions and how they relate to the generalized linear model, of which the probit model is one variant).

Model Building. The nature of probit analysis and why it is appropriate for modeling individual-level turnout has been discussed previously. I will now turn to how specific models useful for studying turnout decline can be constructed.

Before technical details are dealt with, however, the purpose of the model-building process should be examined. The examination should begin with a basic idea: that an investigation seeking to explain change over time in the level of voter participation implicitly starts with a simple model already in place. This model includes only one variable, time, and accurately plots changing turnout levels. The problem is that this model explains nothing in substantive terms, since to ascribe change over time to time is tautological. The simple model, with no variable but time, then, represents a state of complete ignorance about the real cause of turnout decline.

And this state of ignorance is really where the investigation starts. The idea, therefore, is to transform this ignorance into knowledge by adding terms to the model that will capture the variation associated with time in the beginning model. This is the basic purpose of the model-building process.

The mechanics of the model-building process may now be usefully summarized. The first step will be to estimate the "simple" model. This can easily be done by running a probit model that includes only the five dummy variables necessary to represent the six time points in the data set (i.e., one dummy each for 1964, 1968, 1972, 1976, and 1980).

The next step will be adding variables to the model that are believed to be relevant to the question of turnout decline. The first variables added here will be education, occupation, and income. This is because, as discussed earlier, the effect of socioeconomic change on turnout levels should have been to promote, rather than dampen, participation. Thus adding these variables to the model should increase the coefficients of the time dummies, since there will be "more" turnout decline to be explained (and there are no other factors in the model that can do this explaining). Another way of saying this is that education, occupation, and income—especially education—act as suppressor variables on time, so adding SES to the model will allow the "true" effects of time to be discerned.

Other variables will then be inserted into the model to discover the origins of this SES-adjusted decline, represented by the (now larger) coefficients of the time dummies. As these variables are added, the ways in which the time coefficients change will be observed. If these coefficients are significantly decreased by the addition of a given variable, this would be a sign that distributional change on that variable had a substantial role in turnout decline. Further, if the addition of a certain number of variables results in the elimination of the time dummies as significant factors in the model, this would suggest that distributional change on these variables could plausibly account for the fall in participation over the twenty-year period. This latter eventuality would obviously be a desirable result, since it would provide a simple and easily interpretable explanation for turnout decline.

Whatever the results of adding a sequence of variables to the model, however, there is an additional step that should be performed: the consideration of interaction effects between time and the various characteristics in the model. This is because (a) if a significant part of turnout decline has not been explained through the additive process just described (i.e., the coefficients of the time dummies are still substantial), it is possible that some of the remaining decline may be due to changes over time in the effects of variables (see Table 2-1); and (b) even if the influence of time in the model is effectively eliminated, it is still worth checking interaction terms to see whether any of them are substantial. It is possible, for instance, that distributional change on a given variable might be offset by a lessening of that variable's effect.

But how is it to be decided which interaction terms to include in the model? Or, for that matter, which variables from the additive procedure are worth retaining—and categories of these characteristics, if they are considered categorical within the framework of the model? There is, of course, no hard and fast way of making these determinations. That is, there is no one statistical test (or tests) that can be mechanically relied on for such judgments. A decision to include a particular term in a model, or collapse over certain categories for a variable, should be informed by criteria of theoretical plausibility and analytical importance, not just the results of statistical procedures.

With that in mind, there are, nevertheless, two statistical tests that will be of invaluable assistance in making these decisions. The first is the familiar t test, where the coefficient of the variable is divided by its standard error, to see whether that coefficient differs significantly from 0 (at a level of significance designated by the investigator). If it does not, this is good evidence that the relationship between the variable in question and the DV is not important.[1]

The second test is considerably less familiar. It is used to test the relative usefulness of a model but is quite different from the F tests used in OLS regression. F tests are based on the difference in explained sums of squares between models. In probit analysis, however, the explained sum of squares is not a meaningful quantity, since this is not the basis on which parameter estimates are derived. Instead, these estimates are maximum likelihood estimates (MLEs), based on probabilistic criteria that need not detain us here (see Bishop, Feinberg, and Holland 1975, pp. 57–122, for a discussion of MLEs and how they are estimated).

The relevant question for a model based on MLEs is how well the model fits, relative to other models, not explained variance. This may be answered, approximately, with a likelihood statistic called, variously, G-squared, -2 X log-likelihood ratio—which it literally is—or the scaled deviance. I shall use the latter term, since it is the one used by the software package GLIM, which is the most common package used to estimate MLE models and the one I use myself. The scaled deviance measures the goodness-of-fit (GOF) of the model in likelihood terms. The test statistic I have in mind is produced by subtracting the scaled deviance of the full model from that of the simplified, reduced model (the models must be hierarchically nested). This difference is distributed asymptotically as chi-square with degrees of freedom equal to the difference in degrees of freedom between the models (see Baker and Nelder 1978, section 5, and Bishop, Feinberg, and Holland 1975, pp. 123–131, for discussions of this statistic and its strengths and weaknesses).

Just as with a t test or an F test, the level of significance for this statistic is set by the investigator. The value of the statistic is then compared with the appropriate test chi-square value at this level of significance. Lack of significance indicates that relatively little information has been lost by simplifying the model, considering the degrees of freedom that were saved in the process. This provides a reasonable basis for asserting that the relationships between the DV and the variables or categories deleted from the model are not particularly important, and thus can be left out of further analysis.

This concludes the outline of statistical methodologies to be used in this analysis. Given that the basic investigatory framework has been set, it is now appropriate to directly apply these methodologies to analyzing the turnout decline puzzle.

Note

1. In this study I use a criterion of a coefficient being twice its standard error—about a .05 level of significance in the normal distribution. This is despite the fact that, owing to the nature of the standard errors generated when estimating MLEs, it is sometimes advised that coefficients not three times their standard error be regarded with suspicion. Because my interest lies mostly in finding out when terms—like time coefficients—can be confidently judged to be "insignificant," I adopt a conservative bias by making it harder to reach that judgment about the effects of characteristics.

3

Is Demography Destiny? Social Structure and Turnout Decline

Was the fall in voter participation the inevitable fate of a nation undergoing rapid demographic change? If so, a clear and parsimonious story could be told about turnout decline, and its relation to the American electorate. Rather than political disconnection being key, which then needs to be described and accounted for, the crucial change would simply be an extension of the demographic periphery of the system, thereby increasing the proportion of citizens whose background characteristics make electoral participation difficult.

This chapter tests that possibility using the data from the American National Election Studies (ANES) survey (see Appendix for a detailed discussion of this data set). The characteristics examined will be education, occupation, income, age, residential mobility, marital status, race, region, and sex. If social structural changes fail to account for all of the decline in turnout—which seems likely in view of previous findings in the literature—much valuable information will still be gained concerning the relevance of these changes to participation levels. This information may then be used as a basis for pursuing the rest of the analysis.

Social Structure and Turnout

Before the relationship of social structure to turnout decline, in particular, is examined, it is worthwhile to examine the general relationship between social structure and turnout. This subject is pursued below, beginning with the bivariate relationships between voting and different demographic characteristics.

Bivariate Models. Table 3-1 summarizes the results of some models that were run using different sets of demographic characteristics. The first column shows the coefficients for a series of bivariate models, one for each social structural variable described in the previous section. There are several comments worth making about the coefficients displayed there. First, coefficients are not listed for every category in Table 1-1 (this comment is generic to all models described, not just these particular bivariate ones). This is because categorical variables, in analyses of this nature, are represented by sets of dummy variables, where there are N-1 dummies for N categories. The categories that do not have dummy variables are called "reference categories," and the coefficients displayed should be thought of as expressing the effect of a given category, relative to the reference category for that particular variable. Further, in each case, the reference category selected has been the one with the lowest turnout rate, so that the coefficients of different variables will be uniformly signed (positive).

Second, note that the ordering of the coefficients for different variables is as one would expect it. For example, the higher the educational attainment, the greater the coefficient for the category, and hence the higher the probability of voting (all other things being equal). The ordering is analogous for age and occupation.

Third, the results suggest that, on this bivariate level, education is the strongest demographic predictor of turnout. This is indicated, although hardly "proved," by the considerably lower scaled deviance of the education model, relative to all the others. This supports the findings of Wolfinger and Rosenstone on the critical importance of educational attainment as a determinant of turnout. But these are only bivariate relationships, and multivariate models are necessary to make meaningful determinations concerning the relative importance of the relationships between these variables and turnout. These models are considered below.

Multivariate Models. Table 3-2 summarizes the results of the multivariate models, and shows the coefficients of the bivariate models, for purposes of comparison. The first model to be discussed here is the one whose coefficients are displayed in the second column of the table. This is a simple two-variable model that

Table 3-1
Social Structure and Turnout: Bivariate Models

	bivariate coefficient	scaled deviance	degrees of freedom
EDUCATION			
9-11 years	.046	10260	8284
12	.413*		
13-15	.608*		
16 or more	.912*		
AGE			
25-28 years	.227*	10440	8284
29-32	.410*		
33-36	.554*		
37 or more	.653*		
MARITAL STATUS			
married-SP (1)	.335*	10580	8287
RESIDENTIAL MOBILITY			
not mobile (2)	.491*	10460	8287
OCCUPATION			
blue collar (3)	.004	10580	8286
white collar and other	.318*		
FAMILY INCOME			
non-poor (4)	.468*	10440	8287
SEX			
male	.212*	10650	8287
RACE			
white	.428*	10600	8287
REGION			
non-south	.383*	10560	8287

----

(1) SP = spouse present
(2) mobile is defined as within two years
(3) blue collar includes service workers
(4) poor is defined as less than 5000 in 1960 dollars

* = coefficient is at least twice its standard error.

Unweighted N = 8289
Note: Reference categories for variables may be found by referring to Table 1-1. In all cases, they are the first category listed under a particular variable.

Note: Scaled deviance of null model is 10710.

includes only education and age. The interesting thing to note here is the strong suppressor effects that education and age were clearly exerting on each other when the effects of each were estimated on a bivariate basis. For each category of both variables (with the exception of the twenty-five- to twenty-eight-year-old category of age), the estimated effects are stronger when both age and education are present in the model than when each is considered alone. This is apparently caused by the well-known tendency of older people (higher turnout) to have lower educational attainment (lower turnout), so that if the effect of age is estimated without controlling for education, those estimates will be "damped down" by the age distribution of education. Thus age and education must both be present in the model if reasonably accurate estimates of these effects are to be obtained.

The next column of the table shows the coefficients from a model including occupation and income, as well as education and age. The effect on the age coefficients is fairly minimal, but the effect on those for education is substantial. For every category the estimates are substantially smaller, with the attenuation being stronger the higher the educational category. Thus the estimates for education that are displayed in column two are evidently capturing some of the variation really caused by occupation and income. This makes sense, since we know that those with relatively high incomes or in relatively high-status occupations will tend to have higher educational levels.

The same comment is applicable to the attenuation of the occupation and income effects, which may be observed when moving from column one to column three of the table. These effects are much stronger on the bivariate level than in this four-variable model. Again, this makes sense, given what we know of the relationships among education, occupation, and income. Thus, as discussed in the previous section, more accurate estimates for these variables are obtained when all three are present in the model.

The final column of Table 3-2 displays the coefficients from a model including all nine of the demographic variables discussed in the previous section. As can be easily seen, all coefficients are at least twice their standard error, except for the blue-collar category in the occupation variable. It is also worth noting that the scaled deviance of this model is 992 less than the model with education

Table 3-2

Social Structure and Turnout: Coefficients for Bivariate and Multivariate Models

	bivariate	age, education	+income, occupation	all variables
EDUCATION				
9-11 years	.046	.212*	.160*	.176*
12	.413*	.702*	.574*	.587*
13-15	.608*	.982*	.814*	.871*
16 or more	.912*	1.19*	.963*	1.05*
AGE				
25-28 years	.227*	.216*	.193*	.099*
29-32	.410*	.468*	.443*	.295*
33-36	.554*	.611*	.572*	.447*
37 or more	.653*	.961*	.936*	.736*
MARITAL STATUS				
married-SP (1)	.335*			.280*
RESIDENTIAL MOBILITY				
not mobile (2)	.491*			.417*
OCCUPATION				
blue collar (3)	.004		.066	.055
white collar and other	.318*		.212*	.235*
FAMILY INCOME				
non-poor (4)	.468*		.312*	.149*
SEX				
male	.212*			.106*
RACE				
white	.428*			.103*
REGION				
non-south	.383*			.320*
intercept	.333*(5)	-.571*	-.748*	-1.38*
scaled deviance (SD)	10260 (5)	9724	9601	9268
degrees of freedom (DF)	8284 (5)	8280	8277	8272
difference in SD (6)		536**	123**	333**
difference in DF (6)		4	3	5

(1) SP = spouse present
(2) mobile is defined as within two years
(3) blue collar includes service workers
(4) poor is defined as less than 5000 in 1960 dollars
(5) these figures are for the bivariate education model
(6) differences are between the current model and the one immediately previous. The SD difference is distributed approximately as chi-square with degrees of freedom equal to the DF difference between the models (number of extra parameters fitted in the current model).

* = coefficient is at least twice its standard error.
** = chi-square is significant at .05 level.

Unweighted N = 8289
Note: Reference categories for variables may be found by referring to Table 1-1. In all cases, they are the first category listed under a particular variable.

alone, while using up only 12 degrees of freedom. This is obviously a significant increase in GOF, (see chapter 2 for a discussion of the difference in scaled deviance criterion).

The patterning and magnitude of these coefficients deserve several comments. First, the coefficients for education are actually higher in the full social structural model than they were when estimated on the bivariate level. This primarily reflects the suppressor relationship between age and education, but it also shows that the rest of these demographic predictors do not seriously attenuate the powerful effect of education.

Second, although all other coefficients, with the exception of the thirty-seven-or-older category of the age variable, are at least somewhat attenuated when moving from the bivariate to the multivariate level, there is a lot of variation in the level of this attenuation. The income and race coefficients, for instance, decline sharply—by over .3 in each case—going from over .4 to under .2. The sex coefficient also declines substantially, going from .212 to .106, thereby cutting its effect in half. In contrast, variables like mobility, marital status, and region are affected much less by the controls in the full social structural model, thereby indicating that they are relatively orthogonal to one another and to the other characteristics in the model.

Regardless of the extent of attenuation, however—or enhancement in the case of education—it is apparent that better estimates for the effects of these variables are obtained when all are included in the model. The significance of almost all coefficients, as well as the dramatic increase in GOF also suggests the usefulness of the full social structure model in this context. Given these results, it is now appropriate to turn to the relationship between the variables included in this full model and the specific question of turnout decline.

Social Structure and Turnout Decline

Table 3-3 displays the coefficients of the five time dummies for a series of successively more complex turnout models. This series is constructed in such a way that each model is nested within all those models more complex than itself. The first model—first column—consists simply of these five time dummies, with no other variables included. The final model—last column—includes all the social structure variables mentioned previously, as well as the dummies for time period. The idea here, as explained in the discussion of statistical methodologies, is simple: if distributional change on these demographic variables can substantially account for turnout decline, the coefficients of these time dummies should be seriously attenuated by the successive addition of these variables to the model.

The model in the first column does nothing more than fit the means of the dependent variable, turnout, in the different years. Just as we would expect, the coefficients are all negatively signed and increase in magnitude diachronically (i.e., moving through time from 1964 to 1980).

Education. The second column shows the time dummy coefficients when education is added to the model. As would be suspected from previous discussion of the relation of increased educational attainment to turnout levels, these coefficients are dramatically larger than those generated without education in the equation. This means that education exerts a suppressor influence on time when it is not included in the model. Further, because the increase in educational attainment is greater, relative to 1960, the later the time period, the increase in magnitude of the time dummy coefficients is also greater the later the year under consideration. Put simply, then, there is more turnout decline to be explained than before—especially in terms of the key 1960–1980 differential—once the effects of education are taken into account.

Occupation and Income. The next column displays the time coefficients when occupation and income are added to the model. These coefficients are again increased by the addition of more variables to the model, although the magnitude of the increase is far smaller than that produced by the addition of the education variable. This is not surprising in view of the particular variables involved. Both occupation and income experienced distributional shifts over the two-decade time period that decreased the proportions in low turnout categories—fewer blue-collar workers and housewives, fewer "poor" people—thereby increasing the proportions in the higher turnout groupings. The result, as in the case of education, is more turnout decline to be explained, expressed in the increased magnitude of the time coefficients. These coeffi-

Table 3-3

Social Structure and Turnout Decline: Coefficients of Time Dummies in Different Models

	Time Only	+educa-tion	+income, occupa-tion	+age	+mobility, marital status	all vari-ables
YEAR						
1964	-.052	-.085	-.089	-.074	-.060	-.065
1968	-.113*	-.183*	-.189*	-.192*	-.221*	-.224*
1972	-.196*	-.287*	-.306*	-.256*	-.286*	-.276*
1976	-.249*	-.392*	-.405*	-.354*	-.316*	-.311*
1980	-.255*	-.438*	-.465*	-.422*	-.371*	-.353*
intercept	.816*	.524*	.318*	-.539*	-.866*	-1.15*
SD	10660	10130	9977	9503	9304	9198
DF	8283	8279	8276	8272	8270	8267
SD difference (1)		530**	153**	474**	299**	106**
DF difference		4	3	4	2	3
SD minus time(2)	50**	130**	176**	98**	77**	70**

SD = scaled deviance
DF = degrees of freedom

(1) differences are between the current model and the one immediately previous. The SD difference is distributed approximately as chi-square with degrees of freedom equal to the DF difference between the models (number of extra parameters fitted in the current model).

(2) this quantity is the difference in scaled deviance when time is removed from a given model. It is a chi-square statistic with five degrees of freedom.

* = coefficient is at least twice its standard error
** = chi-square is significant at .05 level
_____
Unweighted N = 8289
Note: 1960 is reference category for time variable.

cients, now controlled for the effects of education, occupation, and income, the three components of socioeconomic status (SES), may be thought of as representing the overall SES-adjusted effect of time, and thus the overall SES-adjusted—and greater than observed—amount of turnout decline to be explained.

Age. Thus far the addition of variables to the model has only increased the magnitude of the problem to be solved: the fall in voting participation over the twenty-year period. The next model, one that adds age to the variables already in the equation, reverses this trend. As can be seen from the appropriate column in the table, the time dummy coefficients are markedly decreased by entering age into the equation. This means that distributional change in the age structure of the electorate—increasing youthfulness— over the 1960–1980 time period has been a factor in promoting turnout decline.

The influence of this factor was hardly uniform, however, and this is reflected in the patterning of change evidenced by the coefficients. It is only in 1972 and the later years that distributional change on the age variable makes itself felt. This implies that it was the constitutional-demographic change of 1972, when eighteen- to twenty-year-olds were admitted to the electorate, that is mostly responsible for the role of age in turnout decline.

Residential Mobility and Marital Status. The next column of the table displays the time dummy coefficients for a model in which mobility and marital status have been added to the equation. As was the case with age, some of these coefficients are significantly attenuated by the entry of the new variables. In particular, the 1980 coefficient, which taps the 1960–1980 turnout differential, is markedly decreased, suggesting that distributional change on these two variables—increasing residential mobility, increasing proportion not married and living with spouse—has promoted this differential.

The 1968 and 1972 coefficients are rather puzzling, however. In these cases the coefficients are larger than they were previously. Does this mean that these factors were actually retarding turnout decline during that period? This seems odd in view of the monotonic distributional declines shown for both characteristics in Table 1-1 over the entire two decades. It appears less odd, though, when it is remembered that the 1968 and 1972 mobility proportions in that table are estimated through interpolation and do not correspond to the proportions for these years that are actually present in the data. These proportions, as explained in the Appendix, considerably underestimate the extent of residential mobility in 1968 and 1972, meaning that mobility will actually appear to go down in this period. This is the trend contained in the data, thereby explaining the behavior of the time dummies in these two years. (This data problem should be kept in mind when interpreting the behavior of the 1968 and 1972 time dummies, not just here, but in any model that contains the mobility variable.)

All Social Structure Variables. The final column in the table shows the time coefficients with race, region, and sex added to the model, thereby including all demographic predictors in the equation. As could be anticipated from previous remarks, these three additional variables make little difference to the time dummy estimates, thus indicating that changes in racial, sexual, and regional distribution played little role in turnout decline.

Several additional remarks should be made about the results from this full social structure model. The first is that demographic distributional change clearly cannot be held responsible for the fall in turnout over the 1960–1980 time period. In each year the coefficients of the time dummies in the final model are actually *greater* than those in the initial model—especially the 1980 coefficient, which represents the difference in turnout levels between the end points of the period. This means that there is more turnout decline to be explained, once all social structure variables are taken into account, than there was in the beginning, when only the observed turnout trend over time was modeled. Thus the demographic analysis of turnout decline, at least in distributional terms, has, rather than solving the problem under consideration, simply made it larger.

Another way of interpreting these results is as follows. The addition of education, occupation, and income—particularly education—to the model increased the magnitude of the time dummies. These coefficients represented the SES-adjusted turnout decline to be explained.

Taking this SES-adjusted turnout decline as the target of investigation, it can be seen that demography has played a role in falling voter participation. The addition of the other variables—all the *non*-SES social structural characteristics—does, in fact, reduce the magnitude of the time coefficients from their SES-adjusted level. This may be seen by comparing the column for the full model with that for the model where this adjusted level is reached. Therefore, distributional changes on these characteristics, especially age, mobility, and marital status, have been factors in promoting turnout decline. This is especially notable when looking at the changes in the 1980 coefficient, where there are no data problems, and the full extent of these distributional changes can be realized. This coefficient declines by over .11 between the two models just mentioned, a fairly substantial decrease.

This said, however, the fact remains that most of the SES-adjusted decline has still not been explained. This suggests that other research avenues will have to be pursued if the full story of falling voter participation is to be told. At least one such avenue can be explored without introducing new variables into the analysis. This entails looking at the possible relationship between changes in effects of demographic characteristics over time and decline in turnout. This logical possibility (box 1 in Table 2-1) is discussed below.

Interaction Effects. The basic methodology used here was to estimate interaction effects for all variables for all years and then trim those that did not significantly improve the GOF of the model, by means of the difference in scaled deviance criterion. The results of this procedure—not reported here—proved not to be helpful. Although the GOF of the model was significantly improved (scaled deviance = 100, degrees of freedom = 17), the estimates for the time dummies were not attenuated by the introduction of these (17) interaction effects into the equation. On the contrary, their magnitudes were substantially enhanced, while, at the same time, their signs were reversed. In other words, the time coefficients became both larger and positively signed when the interaction terms were added to the model.

These results are essentially uninterpretable. If taken literally, they would imply that there were unknown factors pushing up turnout in the 1960–1980 time period of a magnitude considerably greater than the level of turnout decline observed over the two decades. Especially since education, occupation, and income are all controlled for in the model already, it is difficult to come up with a plausible explanation for the existence of these unknown factors, let alone devise a way of identifying them. Given this, and the possibility that some of these interaction effects may be capturing variation caused by other characteristics not currently included in the model, further discussion of interaction effects will be postponed until this possibility is explored.[1]

Summary

In this chapter, nine variables were introduced into the investigation: education, occupation, income, age, marital status, residential mobility, race, region, and sex. These variables were used to construct a social structural model of turnout, which was then applied to the specific question of turnout decline.

The inquiry into the role of demography in decreased participation revealed the following. First, it was found that distributional changes over time on the education, occupation, and income variables all functioned to promote, rather than depress, turnout. This meant that there was actually more turnout decline to be accounted for, once these variables were controlled for, than was apparent from the observed trends in turnout levels. This SES-adjusted decline, it was pointed out, constituted the real target for analytical efforts—the fall in turnout whose origins must be fully accounted for to solve the problem under consideration.

Subsequent investigation showed that distributional changes on the age, mobility, and marital status variables could be held accountable for at least some of this SES-adjusted decline. That is, increased youthfulness, mostly after 1968, increased mobility, and increased proportion not married and living with spouse were all changes among the electorate that played roles in decreased voter participation—especially in terms of the 1960–1980 turnout differential.

Put more generally, it has now been shown, on the one hand, that Americans became more "middle class" between 1960 and 1980, and that this change should have encouraged participation. On the other hand, it has also been shown that Americans became less socially "rooted," and this change discouraged participation. Thus the social structure that underpinned the system of the 1950s changed significantly, but in opposite "directions," as far as effect on turnout was concerned.

Precisely because of this it was found that distributional changes in the social structure could not explain most of the *SES-adjusted* decline in turnout. In fact, once all demographic characteristics had been controlled for in the additive model, there was still more turnout decline—greater effects of time—to be accounted for than when the investigation began and the effect of time alone was modeled. This means that the estimated net effect of social structural change was to promote, rather than depress, turnout. At this stage of the investigation, therefore, it appears that the demographic core of the American electorate expanded, rather than contracted. Voting, on balance, became easier for Americans, rather than more difficult.

The nature of these results indicates that other possible causes of falling voter participation must be introduced into the analysis. This entails the addition of new variables to the social structural turnout model just developed. Such variables will tap different ways in which the political periphery of the system may have expanded—that is, ways in which aggregate political change may have made electoral participation less meaningful for Americans. These sociopolitical variables are introduced and analyzed in the next chapter.

Note

1. It should be pointed out here that other interaction effects were looked at besides those between demographic predictors and time dummies. For instance, interaction effects between age and education were examined as a further test for possible changes in the salience of education to turnout. Other theoretically plausible interactions, like those between sex and occupation, and between race and income, were also estimated. None of these interactions proved to be important, by GOF or other criteria.

4

Beyond Demography:
The Politics of Turnout Decline

[I] couldn't say that man was right and that man wrong. . . .
In a way I feel that what politicians do is none of my busi-
ness. . . . It all seems sort of foreign. It's all media-oriented.
It's like selling toothpaste.

—Twenty-three-year-old nonvoter,
quoted in Hadley (1978)

The results of the previous chapter showed that turnout decline in
the 1960–1980 period could not be substantially attributed to social structural change. This chapter looks at the other set of factors possibly relevant to decreased turnout: those tapping the connections of individuals to the political system—what I have called
sociopolitical characteristics. The three characteristics to be examined are partisanship, political efficacy, and campaign newspaper reading. Analyzing their relationship to turnout decline will
test the possibility that the key change lay in the disconnection of
individuals from politics—the erosion of certain attitudinal/
behavioral commitments to the political system—which made
elections less meaningful for Americans.[1]

Social Structure, Sociopolitical Characteristics and Turnout

Table 4-1 shows the results when the three sociopolitical variables are successively added to the full social structure turnout

model. As can be seen from the difference in the scaled deviance row of the table, each of these variables substantially improves the goodness of fit of the model. This indicates that all three socio-political characteristics have effects on turnout that are independent of those traceable to an individual's demographic position.

The second column displays the coefficients of variables after the first characteristic, partisanship, is added to the model. There are several things worth noting about these results: (a) A number of the parameter estimates are essentially unaffected by the presence of partisanship, including, interestingly enough, those for the education variable. This indicates that previous estimates for these variables were not capturing, through intercorrelation, any of the effect on turnout actually attributable to partisanship. (b) Partisanship was evidently exerting a suppressor effect on income and race, since these estimates go up when the former variable is added to the model. This means that nonwhites and poor people tend to be more highly partisan than whites and the nonpoor, respectively. (c) The estimates for the age coefficients go down significantly when partisanship is added to the model. This indicates that older people tend to be more partisan, so previous estimates of age's effect had captured some of the effect on turnout properly attributable to partisanship.

The third column presents a model in which political efficacy is added to the model just described. The estimates most affected by the addition of this characteristic are those for the education variable. They are substantially attenuated, indicating a strong correlation between efficacy and education (i.e., the higher educational levels have higher levels of political efficacy). Most other estimates are moderately attenuated, although some, like mobility, occupation, and sex, are essentially unchanged. In addition, there appears to have been a weak suppressor relationship between age and efficacy, with the estimates for most age groups becoming somewhat higher with efficacy in the equation. This indicates that the youngest age group tends to be slightly more efficacious than these other groups.

The final column adds the newspaper reading variable to the model. The resultant estimates for partisanship and efficacy are modestly attenuated, indicating some positive correlation between these characteristics and newspaper reading. In addition, as one

Table 4-1

Social Structure, Sociopolitical Characteristics, and Turnout: Coefficients of Variables in Multivariate Models

	all social structure	+partisan- ship	+efficacy	+newspaper reading
EDUCATION (1)				
12 years	.496*	.521*	.457*	.396*
13-15	.779*	.781*	.672*	.566*
16 or more	.961*	.965*	.836*	.690*
AGE				
25-28 years	.097	.074	.093	.065
29-32	.294*	.259*	.271*	.214*
33-36	.444*	.387*	.380*	.316*
37 or more	.712*	.615*	.634*	.535*
MARITAL STATUS				
married-SP	.280*	.284*	.259*	.229*
RESIDENTIAL MOBILITY				
not mobile	.417*	.413*	.421*	.422*
OCCUPATION				
blue collar	.064	.071	.062	.058
white collar and other	.240*	.233*	.233*	.220*
FAMILY INCOME				
non-poor	.165*	.194*	.157*	.141*
SEX				
male	.092*	.094*	.095*	.060*
RACE				
white	.108*	.180*	.160*	.107*
REGION				
non-south	.319*	.315*	.296*	.296*
PARTISANSHIP				
interval scale (2)		.454*	.419*	.383*
POLITICAL EFFICACY				
interval scale (2)			.291*	.254*
NEWSPAPER READING				
some articles				.321*
many articles				.577*
intercept	-1.29*	-1.81*	-1.98*	-1.98*
scaled deviance (SD)	9283	8933	8695	8484
degrees of freedom (DF)	8273	8272	8271	8269
difference in SD		350**	238**	211**
difference in DF		1	1	2

(1) 0-8 and 9-11 years of education have been combined, since no significant difference was found between these categories when the socio-political variables were controlled for.

(2) These scales are both 0,1,2 scales. Their derivations are discussed at the beginning of the current chapter.

* = coefficient is at least twice its standard error.
** = chi-square is significant at .05 level.

Unweighted N = 8289
Note: Reference categories (except for education) and definitions of categories are the same as in Table 3-2.

might expect, the education estimates drop sharply, with the drop being greater the higher the educational level. This means that as education increases, the amount of campaign newspaper reading does as well. The age estimates display the same pattern, showing that growing older also increases the extent to which campaigns are followed in the papers.

The largest decreases for other estimates are for the sex and race variables. The coefficient for sex actually declines to the point where it is, by usual t test criteria, statistically insignificant. Other estimates are slightly attenuated or, like mobility and region, essentially unchanged.

In conclusion, the addition of the three sociopolitical characteristics to the turnout model decreases the scaled deviance by almost 800, while fitting only four parameters. This is a large increase in goodness of fit, considering the small number of degrees of freedom used up. These characteristics may therefore be assumed to be important determinants of an individual's likelihood of voting.

Social Structure, Sociopolitical Characteristics, and Turnout Decline

This section follows the same procedure used in the previous chapter for examining the relationship between turnout decline and variables newly introduced into the model. Variables will be added to a model that initially includes all characteristics examined previously (in this case, the nine social structural attributes), plus the five dummy variables representing time period. These dummies will then be examined, both for the pattern and magnitude of changes, so that the role of sociopolitical characteristics in turnout decline can be assessed. If the coefficients of the time dummies are attenuated to the point where they are statistically insignificant, this would indicate that, with the addition of these characteristics, adjusted turnout decline has largely been accounted for.

Table 4-2 displays the time dummy estimates for a series of turnout models that include these dummies. The first column shows the model with time only. These estimates model the decline in turnout as it was reported in the data. The second column reports the coefficients for a model including all demographic variables. As discussed in the previous chapter, the estimates here represent the net amount of turnout decline that remains unexplained, once the upward push from socioeconomic upgrading is balanced against the downward pressure from other sources of social structural change.

The third column shows the time coefficients when the partisanship variable is added to the equation. Except in the case of 1964, these coefficients are markedly smaller than they were in the previous model. This indicates that distributional change on this variable can explain some of the adjusted turnout decline not accounted for by demographic change. It is still true, however, that the estimated effect of time is higher than in the initial model that included no individual attributes. Thus the puzzle is far from solved by the addition of the partisanship variable.

The next column reports the results when political efficacy is added to the model. These results are striking. The addition of this single variable drastically reduces the time estimates, especially from 1968 on. None of the estimates are above .2 and only two are above .1 (and one of these two is just barely above that level). This contrasts with the previous model, in which three and four estimates, respectively, were above these levels. The seriousness of these changes is underscored by the fact that only the 1980 coefficient remains statistically significant by t test criteria. In addition, removing time from the model increases the scaled deviance by only 7—an insignificant amount—indicating that time has lost most of its ability to predict the likelihood of turnout. It is fair to conclude, therefore, that (a) the decline in political efficacy can be held responsible for a substantial portion of adjusted turnout decline during the 1960–1980 time period, and (b) adjusted turnout decline itself is close to being accounted for.

The fifth column shows the time dummy estimates when the last sociopolitical characteristic, campaign newspaper reading, is added to the model. These results are also quite striking. The estimates after 1968 all decline by a factor of .1 or more, and all of the time estimates are now considerably under the .1 level.[2] The 1980 coefficient, in particular, is under .05 and no longer has a statistically significant t test. It is thus evident that the decline in campaign newspaper reading is also an important factor in explaining declining turnout.

In addition, the increase in scaled deviance produced by remov-

Table 4-2

Social Structure, Sociopolitical Characteristics, and Turnout Decline: Coefficients of Time Dummies in Different Models

YEAR	Time only	Time, all demo- graphic	+partisan- ship	+effi- cacy	+news- paper reading	inter- active model
1964	-.052	-.057	-.086	-.039	-.040	-.020
1968	-.113*	-.217*	-.196*	-.074	-.061	----
1972	-.196*	-.267*	-.218*	-.104	.004	.283*
1976	-.249*	-.300*	-.240*	-.084	-.032	.283*
1980	-.255*	-.338*	-.296*	-.140*	-.047	----
intercept	.816*	-1.06*	-1.59*	-1.88*	-1.96*	-2.12*

	Time only	demographic	partisanship	efficacy	newspaper	interactive
SD	10660	9216	8893	8688	8482	8409
DF	8283	8268	8267	8266	8264	8261
SD difference (1)		1444**	323**	205**	206**	(2)
DF difference (1)		15	1	1	2	(2)
SD minus time (3)		70**	40**	7	2	----

SD = scaled deviance
DF = degrees of freedom

(1) differences are between the current model and the one immediately previous. The SD difference is distributed approximately as chi-square with degrees of freedom equal to the DF difference between the models (number of extra parameters fitted in the current model).
(2) previous model is not hierarchically nested within current model.
(3) this quantity is the difference in scaled deviance when time is removed from a given model. It is a chi-square statistic with five degrees of freedom.

* = coefficient is at least twice its standard error
** = chi-square is significant at .05 level

Unweighted N=8289; 1960 is reference category for time variable.

ing time from the model is now only two. This indicates that at this point in the modeling process, the explanatory power of time is small indeed. Thus the effect originally estimated for time, which reflected the differences in turnout levels across elections, has now been absorbed by other variables in the model.

These results therefore suggest that the three sociopolitical characteristics just introduced into the model can explain most of adjusted turnout decline not attributable to demographic factors. This means that even with the turnout-promoting effect of SES-upgrading taken into consideration, a combination of social structural and sociopolitical change can largely account for the fall in participation over the two decades in question (an estimate of the extent of this accounting will be offered shortly).

Interaction Effects. The last model to be considered here includes significant interaction effects between variables in the previous model and dummies representing time period. The procedure used in developing this model was the same as that described in chapter 3. All possible interaction effects were considered, and then the unimportant ones eliminated, by means of the difference in scaled deviance criterion. The purpose of the procedure was to check the possibility that changes over time in the effects of characteristics—particularly for race, region, and sex, where there were some substantive reasons to expect such changes—had played a role in turnout decline. The findings described above suggest that distributional changes were the key factors in falling participation, but the possibility was checked anyway.[3]

As indicated in the last column of Table 4-2, the interactive model does not include time dummies for the 1968 and 1980 time periods. These parameters were not fitted, since no significant difference was found between these time periods and 1960, in terms of the effect of any variable. Thus the model was collapsed over time by making 1960, 1968, and 1980 equivalent within the framework of the model (no time dummies or interaction effects for the latter two years). In addition, while 1972 and 1976 showed some differences with the base year of 1960, they showed no significant differences with one another. Thus 1972 and 1976 were collapsed into a single time period, with one time dummy representing the two years and used in interaction terms with appropriate variables.

Six interaction terms were fitted, two positively signed and four negatively signed (estimates not shown). The two positive terms were for region in 1964 and some college in 1972–1976. Thus, according to this model, the effects of being outside the South and having some college were larger in 1964 and 1972–1976, respectively, than in the 1960–1968–1980 elections. The negative terms were for college education and efficacy in 1964 and for race and efficacy in 1972–1976. According to the model, then, the effects of having completed college and being white were less in 1964 and 1972–1976, respectively, than in the years of 1960–1968–1980. The effect of a given level of political efficacy was estimated to be less in both 1964 and 1972–1976 than in the base years just mentioned.[4]

These effects are generally difficult to interpret. There seems to be no compelling reason, for instance, why the effect of efficacy should be different in 1964 than in, say, 1968. Or why the effect of being outside the South should be different in 1964 than in all other years. Other interactions seem somewhat more interpretable. For example, the increased effect of some college in 1972–1976 might be traceable to the galvanizing effect of the 1972 McGovern campaign on college students. Or the decreased negative effect of being nonwhite in 1972–1976 might be due to a mobilization of blacks into electoral politics, perhaps as a follow-up to the riots of the late 1960s. Why such a mobilization would not be relevant to 1980, however, is hard to understand. At any rate, these interpretations are necessarily speculative and hard to document.

These difficulties are underscored by the time dummy estimates shown in the last column of Table 4-2. Whereas the estimate for 1964 is so low ($-.020$) that it presents no real interpretive difficulty, that for the 1972–1976 time period is so high ($+.283$) that it does. This estimate implies that when the interaction effects described above are taken into account, there are unidentified forces pushing up turnout in this period by an amount considerably greater than the level of turnout decline originally observed in the data. Countervailing forces of such magnitude are certainly possible, but given that the increase in educational attainment has already been taken into account, there are no theoretically plausible reasons for supposing that such forces existed—especially only during this period and no other.

Because the results of this interactive model are (a) so difficult to interpret, (b) actually make it harder to explain declining turnout, and (c) seem implausible theoretically, the model does not appear to be a useful one. Thus, even though this model fits somewhat better than the final additive model (scaled deviance is 73 less, while fitting three more parameters—note, though, that the models are not hierarchically nested), the parameter estimates derived from it will not be used in subsequent analysis. Instead, because the additive model explains most of the fall in participation and is easily interpretable, the estimates from this model will be used to analyze turnout decline in more detail.

Decomposing Turnout Decline. It is now appropriate to answer two questions: (1) What is the nature of the story being told by the best model available? According to the model, which factors are responsible for how much of the fall in turnout? (2) How well does the model explain the decline in turnout over the period in question? What proportion of this decline can the variables in the model account for?

These questions will be answered using the additive model just alluded to. This is the model that includes all the variables discussed so far: nine social structural and the three sociopolitical ones introduced in this chapter. The model will not include the time dummies, since they represent unexplained variation in turnout levels, and hence are not relevant to either of the two questions.[5]

The decline in turnout covered will be that for the entire period. This entails looking at the turnout differential between the two years that form the end points of the period: 1960 and 1980. Although other differentials could be examined, this is the most important one and will be looked at first, as has been the practice in the rest of the turnout decline literature (Abramson and Aldrich, Cassel and Hill, Shaffer, etc.). I emphasize, however, that this is not the last step in partitioning turnout decline—as has also been the practice in the literature, unfortunately. There are other parts of the story that cannot be told simply by looking at the 1960–1980 differential, and they will not be neglected in this analysis.

The decomposition of the turnout differential between 1960 and 1980 was accomplished by first substituting the 1960 means of the independent variables into the model (coefficients displayed in the last column of Table 4-1), then the 1980 means, and then subtracting the first set of terms from the second. This produces the three equations show below.

$$\bar{y}_{60} = a + \Sigma b_i(\bar{x}_{60})_i \tag{1}$$
$$\bar{y}_{80} = a + \Sigma b_i(\bar{x}_{80})_i \tag{2}$$
$$\bar{y}_{60} - \bar{y}_{80} = \Sigma b_i((\bar{x}_{60})_i - (\bar{x}_{80})_i) \tag{3}$$

The left side of equation (3) represents the difference in predicted probit between 1960 and 1980. The right side parcels out this difference by variables entered in the model. For each variable there is a term that multiplies the coefficient for that variable by the difference in means for the variable between 1960 and 1980. This represents the contribution of that particular characteristic, or category of a characteristic, to the overall difference in predicted probit, and thus to the 1960–1980 turnout differential predicted by the model.

Finally, the overall probits generated for 1960 and 1980—left side of equations (1) and (2)—can be translated into percentages to get the predicted turnout levels for the two elections. The difference between the 1960 and 1980 figures represents the percentage of decline in turnout predicted by the model. This can then be compared with the decline observed in the data to see what proportion of this decline is accounted for by the model.

The results of this sequence of steps are shown in Table 4-3. The first two columns of the table display the predicted probit decline and the percentage of overall predicted probit decline attributable to a given characteristic, or set of characteristics. These characteristics are divided into three groups: SES characteristics, non-SES demographic characteristics, and sociopolitical characteristics. Each of these groups is worth commenting on separately.

The first group, SES characteristics, consists of education and a category combining occupation and income. All quantities are negatively signed, indicating that these characteristics made negative contributions to turnout decline (i.e., actually served to promote, rather than depress, turnout levels). Education is far and away the crucial factor here, its influence being more than three times as great as occupation and income put together. This is as would be expected, given the superior strength of education as a

Table 4-3

Explaining the Turnout Differential Between 1960 and 1980

variable	predicted decline	% of predicted decline	% of SES-adjusted decline
SOCIO-ECONOMIC CHARACTERISTICS			
education	-.127	-50.3	----
occupation, income	-.039	-15.4	----
all SES	-.166	-65.7	----
NON-SES DEMOGRAPHIC CHARACTERISTICS			
age	.066	26.2	15.8
marital status	.045	17.8	10.7
residential mobility	.033	13.0	7.9
race, region, sex	.014	5.5	3.3
all non-SES demographic	.158	62.5	37.7
SOCIO-POLITICAL CHARACTERISTICS			
partisanship	.046	18.2	11.0
newspaper reading	.104	41.1	24.8
political efficacy	.111	43.9	26.5
all socio-political	.261	103.2	62.3
TOTAL PROBIT DROP	.253	100.0	100.0

percentage point decline in turnout predicted by probit model: 7.0
percentage point decline in turnout reported in ANES survey : 8.0
percent of turnout differential explained by model : 87.5

predictor of turnout and the larger amount of distributional change on this variable over the time period.

Together, the SES characteristics increased the predicted probit by .166, 65.7 percent, in magnitude, of the total probit drop. Translated into percentage terms, this means that, had all other factors remained constant, SES-upgrading would have increased turnout by 3.9 percent. This is nearly half of the turnout decline reported in the data (8 percent), making these countervailing forces substantial ones indeed.

The second group of characteristics includes all demographic characteristics except the socioeconomic ones just mentioned. The three characteristics that make substantial contributions are listed separately—marital status, residential mobility, and age—while the three that make minor contributions are combined into a single category (race, region, sex). Age, according to the model, plays the strongest role in turnout decline, accounting for more than a quarter of the drop in predicted probit. Marital status and mobility account for, respectively, about 18 percent and 13 percent each. Finally, race, region, and sex, as a group, explain less than 6 percent of the drop.[6]

All the non-SES demographic characteristics together decreased the predicted probit by .158, or about 63 percent of the drop predicted by the model. Thus distributional change on these variables made a strong contribution to declining participation. Interestingly, this contribution to turnout decline from non-SES social structural sources is just about equal in magnitude to the upward push on turnout from the SES sources.

The final group of characteristics consists of the three sociopolitical variables introduced in this chapter: partisanship, political efficacy, and campaign newspaper reading. Partisanship plays the weakest role of the three in turnout decline, accounting for about 18 percent of the predicted probit drop. Efficacy and newspaper reading, on the other hand, play strong and roughly equal roles in turnout decline—about 44 percent and 41 percent of total probit drop, respectively. Together, the three variables account for over 100 percent of the decline predicted by the model.

These results are rearranged in the next column. This rearrangement uses the concept of SES-adjusted turnout decline developed earlier. To reflect the fact that SES upgrading served to promote turnout, and thus made the amount of turnout decline to be explained larger than that observed in the data, the predicted probit increase from these characteristics (.166) is added to the overall probit drop (.253) to produce the amount of probit decline actually explained by the other, non-SES variables in the model (.453). The probit drop from individual characteristics, or sets of characteristics, is then divided by .453 to find the proportion of adjusted decline accounted for by these variables. These proportions are what is shown in column three.

These figures make the findings from the decomposition somewhat more intelligible. Here the positive contributions to turnout decline add up to 100 percent, rather than well over 100 percent, as in the previous column. As can be seen from the table, these contributions now break down into 62 percent from sociopolitical sources and 38 percent from non-SES demographic sources. This is roughly a 5:3 ratio.

These results cast some interesting light on previous research into this topic. Abramson and Aldrich, for instance, attributed about two-thirds of the 1960–1980 turnout differential to the combined effects of partisanship and efficacy. Looking at the decomposition of nonadjusted, or net, turnout decline in Table 4-3 (column two), these two variables account for about 62 percent of decline—a comparable figure. However, these two characteristics, considered in the context of the *adjusted* fall in turnout, only explain 37.5 percent of the drop, a less impressive figure. This illustrates how an overly simple model can appear to come close to solving the puzzle, but only does so at the price of serious incompleteness. Once the incompleteness is rectified, as above, it becomes clear that what seemed fairly close to a solution was actually rather far away.

In contrast to previous research, then, the model developed here presents a solution that (a) despite taking into account the true extent of the puzzle, by controlling for socioeconomic upgrading, (b) still does an equally good, or even better, job of solving it. Within the context created by this SES-upgrading, it becomes apparent that factors such as age, newspaper reading, marital status, and mobility must be considered *in addition to* partisanship and efficacy if the fall in turnout is to be adequately explained. Looked at in this way, each of the variables becomes a piece of the puzzle's solution, all of which must be put together to form a complete solution. Two or three pieces cannot stand alone. This is the essence of the story being directly told by the model.

Thus far the discussion has been focused on answering the first question asked about the decomposition: how does it allot responsibility among the different factors influencing turnout decline? But this accounting procedure is essentially internal to the model. It is now appropriate to answer the second question: what proportion of observed turnout decline can be explained by the variables in the model? This measures the model against the crucial external standard by which its usefulness can be judged.

These results are summarized at the bottom of Table 4-3. The fall in turnout predicted by the model is 7 percent, whereas the decline observed in the data is 8 percent. This means that the model accounts for about 88 percent of turnout decline, even with SES-upgrading controlled for. This compares favorably with figures reported by other researchers (Shaffer 1981; Abramson and Aldrich 1982), despite the "advantages" these analysts had by not controlling for upgrading. Thus not only is the model thorough in the range of factors considered, but its predictions are able to explain almost all of the observed decline in turnout as well.

Additional Interpretation. The results presented in Table 4-3 may be further interpreted in the following way. There were really three processes of change taking place between 1960 and 1980, which correspond to the three divisions within the table. First, there was socioeconomic upgrading, which made America, in the popular view, more of a "middle-class" society. This apparently facilitated access to the electoral arena, just as would be expected from the standard literature on turnout. But this was not the only change taking place. While the electorate was becoming more "middle-class," it was also becoming younger, more mobile, and more likely to be single. This decline in the social "rootedness" of the electorate made it harder, in the aggregate, for Americans to handle the voting process. The impact of the two processes of change, as can be seen in column two of Table 4-3, was similar in magnitude, so they roughly canceled each other out. Voting, therefore, became neither significantly easier nor significantly harder as a result of social structural change over the two decades.

The final set of changes involved the links of Americans to their political system. A process of disconnection took place that weakened the individual-level commitments of citizens to the political system and political action. This disconnection made elections less meaningful for voters, thereby weakening their motivation to vote. Unlike the other two processes of change, however, there was nothing to counterbalance the effects of this process. The resultant, therefore, of the three types of changes was the depression in turnout levels over the twenty-year time period.

The imagery of core and periphery provides a helpful way of reformulating this point. If there is both a demographic and a political core of the population, relative to the electoral system, then it may be said that one of these cores—the demographic one—remained about the same between 1960 and 1980. The political core, on the other hand, shrank, owing to the process of disconnection just mentioned. Thus, although the demographic core was stable, the political periphery expanded. This political peripheralization may be viewed as the driving force behind the decline of turnout in the United States.

Conclusion

This chapter began by examining the role of sociopolitical characteristics in turnout decline. It was found that the addition of three variables, partisanship, political efficacy, and campaign newspaper reading, to the social structural model developed previously allowed for the successful elimination of significant effects attributable to time (i.e., effects on turnout levels not traceable to variables included in the analysis). This meant that within the framework of the model, adjusted turnout decline had substantially been accounted for.

An interactive model was also estimated, to see if interaction effects were of importance in explaining turnout decline. Although some significant interaction effects were found, these effects, as well as the new estimates for the time parameters, were found to be basically uninterpretable, and thus not useful for analyzing decreased participation. For this reason the additive model, which included the nine social structural and three sociopolitical variables, was used as a basis for decomposing predicted turnout decline and comparing predicted to observed decline.

This decomposition, based on the 1960–1980 turnout differential, revealed that the upward pressure on voting levels from SES—primarily educational—upgrading was strong, amounting to about two-thirds of total probit decline predicted by the model. This meant that because (a) families had more real income, (b) occupational shifts lowered the proportions of housewives and blue-collar workers, (c) educational attainment went up dramatically, turnout—had nothing else changed save the distribution of the popu-

lation into socioeconomic categories—would have gone up substantially instead of decreasing.

Taking this fact into consideration, it was found that six changes
in American society were largely responsible for the difference in
turnout levels between the 1960 and 1980 elections. The first three
had to do with the decline in the extent to which the electorate
was socially rooted: (1) the voting pool in 1980 was younger than
in 1960; (2) the proportion of the population living "traditionally"—that is, married and living with their spouses—was much
smaller in 1980 than in 1960; and (3) citizens were more mobile
in 1980 than in 1960. Together, these changes accounted for about
38 percent or three-eighths, of the turnout differential between
these two years.

The other three societal changes tapped ways through which
individuals were linked to the political system and political action:
(1) through party identification—voters were less partisan in 1980
than at the beginning of the period; (2) through campaign involvement—a far smaller proportion of the electorate in 1980 followed
the campaign in the newspapers than did in 1960; and (3) through
a belief in the effectiveness of political action—people felt less efficacious, or powerful, relative to governmental actions and public
officials in 1980 than in the earlier year. Together, the erosion of
these political ties accounted for about 62 percent, or five-eighths,
of the difference in turnout levels between 1960 and 1980.

Research Directions. The results presented in this chapter represent a good first step in decoding the turnout decline puzzle.
There are several more questions, however, that need to be answered before the research agenda of the present work is fulfilled.
First, there is the question of the periodization of the turnout decline process. So far, only the differential between the 1960 and
1980 elections has been examined. Were the investigation to stop
here, the implication would be that the relative weights assigned
different factors in analyzing the 1960–1980 differential are the
same throughout the twenty-year time span. Research results presented earlier suggest that this is not a warranted assumption. Declining political efficacy, for instance, seemed to become important
only after 1964, whereas changes in the age distribution and declining newspaper reading really only made themselves felt in the
1972 election and thereafter. These observations alone indicate a

need to look beyond the 1960–1980 turnout differential to a more elaborate periodization of the fall in turnout.

Another unanswered question has to do with the origins of the sociopolitical changes that have played such a key role in explaining decreased participation. Although the social structural changes alluded to here need little elaboration, since they are matters of demographic—or, in the case of age, partially constitutional—fact, these political alterations cannot be considered in the same light. This is because there are ways in which these changes might have come about that would have substantive implications for the research findings.

It is possible, for instance, that these political changes are the indirect product of social structural change. This would mean that although demographic change cannot directly account for turnout decline, it changed the political profile of Americans in such a way as to be indirectly responsible for the decline. In this sense, demographic change, despite the nature of research findings presented thus far, could still prove to be the "driving force" behind the fall in voter turnout.

This possibility and some others will be looked at. The basic idea is to determine, to the extent that this is feasible, whether sociopolitical change represents a historically rooted process of political disconnection, or a reflection of other kinds of social change. This will allow the research results to be interpreted with more confidence.

These two topics—periodizing turnout decline and investigating the origins of sociopolitical change—therefore provide a useful basis for enriching the findings presented so far. They constitute the agenda of the next chapter.

Notes

1. Not only political changes affect the meaningfulness of elections. They just do so more directly. A decline in educational attainment, for instance, would—through a decrease in the ability to handle cognitive tasks—wind up having an effect on the meaningfulness of voting. The difference between this effect and that of a political change is that it is farther up the "funnel of causality," to use the terminology of *The American Voter*.

Although this is an important difference—and what the distinctions between the types of variables is partially getting at—it is nevertheless true that demographic and sociopolitical change cannot be disaggregated on a fundamental theoretical level, once indirect effects are taken into account. They both affect the costs and benefits of voting in complex ways. For descriptive purposes, however, it is essential to keep the effects of the two kinds of changes separate. Otherwise, the most important patterns in the research results will be missed.

2. Note that the time dummy coefficient for 1968 is the greatest in magnitude. This partially reflects the problem with the mobility variable, where the proportion mobile in the data is considerably lower for 1968 and 1972 than the actual population proportions. This means that the time estimates for these years are more negative (by at least .03) than they should be. With this taken into account, the magnitude of the 1968 coefficient is no longer so anomalous. It should also be noted, however, that taking account of this factor would indicate that the 1972 estimate should be at least + .03, making 1972 somewhat different from the other years.

3. Several charcteristic-year interactions were tested for variables not included in the basic model described in the text. For example, citizen duty—a trait that did not change at all distributionally—was checked for a change in effect over time, since such a change was potentially relevant to turnout decline. Neither this interaction nor others tested improved the fit of turnout models enough to suggest such relevance.

4. The six interaction terms here are eleven fewer than the number fitted for the social structural model (17). This suggests that the interaction terms for the previous model may indeed have been capturing some of the variation because of characteristics—like partisanship, efficacy, and newspaper reading—that were not included in the model.

5. The increase in scaled deviance from eliminating the five time parameters is only 2, as pointed out elsewhere in the text. This further justifies the elimination of these parameters from the model used for the decomposition.

6. It is also possible that this 6 percent considerably overestimates the contribution from this category. In Table 1-1 the proportion nonwhite seems unusually high, relative to the figures for the other years. This may reflect measurement error (or, really, its decline), since the question on race for 1980 was a different and more thorough one than in the previous surveys. Thus the increase in proportion nonwhite in the data may be somewhat inflated—and therefore the contribution of racial distributional change to turnout decline inflated as well.

5

The American Nonvoter, 1960–1980: A Closer Look

This chapter builds on the findings discussed previously, so as to give a more detailed portrait of the turnout decline phenomenon. The first topic addressed will be that of periodizing the fall in turnout. At this point it is known that a number of factors had an impact on turnout levels, and therefore played roles in the phenomenon of turnout decline. These include, among others, education, age, partisanship, political efficacy, and campaign newspaper reading. But it is not known at this point which factors were most important in which periods. A periodization of turnout decline will allow this to be determined.

The other topic to be discussed in the chapter concerns the origins of sociopolitical change. The decreases in partisanship, efficacy, and newspaper reading have all been important parts of the story told thus far. But relatively little has been said about why these changes might have occurred. An examination of competing explanations for these changes will shed some light on this matter, and thereby some light on the turnout decline process in general.

Periodizing Turnout Decline

The first question to be answered here is which years are most appropriate to use to divide the twenty-year period into segments. In what follows, I will use the year 1968 to create two segments: 1960–1968 and 1968–1980. There are two reasons for doing this.

The first is rooted in the findings of the previous chapter, in which an interactive model for turnout was estimated. This model revealed the following: (a) no significant interaction or time effects distinguished 1960, 1968, and 1980 from one another; (b) in 1964, 1972, and 1976, however, there were both differences in effects of characteristics and time effects that clouded the picture. The uninterpretability of these interaction effects and the large magnitude of the time effects implied that the basic additive model, despite the improvement in fit from estimating the interactive model, remained the most useful for analyzing turnout decline.

These results also imply, though, that there may be unknown factors affecting turnout levels in 1964, 1972, and 1976. It therefore makes sense, when segmenting the period for further decompositions, to base this segmentation on the three years—1960, 1968, and 1980—where no hints of such unknown factors affecting turnout levels were found. This suggests the periodization, 1960–1968 and 1968–1980.

The second reason bolsters this first, methodological point. A periodization of these two decades that divides the interval at the 1968 election also has substantive motivation. This is because of the magnitude of change in the American political universe after 1968. Some examples: protest movements ceased to dominate the headlines and set the political tenor for the entire country; campaign practices changed drastically, with astounding amounts of time and money poured into the use of television (Sabato 1981); a constitutional amendment gave eighteen- to twenty-year-olds the right to vote; Watergate happened and Nixon resigned. In short, the 1960s (as a politically, not just chronologically, defined period of time) gave way to the 1970s. This change is captured (as well as one can using a set of elections spaced four years apart) by the 1960–1968 and 1968–1980 periodization. Thus if the net trends detailed in Table 4-3 were not uniform and had differential impact over the two decades, such differences can be expected to show themselves, in some form, by means of this periodization.

1960–1968. 1960 was the year John Kennedy got elected, with the highest voter turnout since 1908. A mood of political optimism swept the country, with Kennedy's youth and vigor seeming to promise a fresh, daring approach to social and global problems (the "New Frontier").

This optimism died down considerably before the end of this period, however. To begin with, of course, John Kennedy was assassinated after three years of his presidency. Even before that, complex issues of war and peace had come to the fore (the Cuban missile crisis) and later became the centerpiece of the 1964 contest between Goldwater and Johnson. The civil rights movement also stirred and grew, culminating in the black riots that swept the country in 1968. Then there was the youth and student movement, centered around protest against the Vietnam war, which developed into a strong social force affecting both those who identified with it and those who opposed it. In addition, this era saw the beginnings of a women's movement, as well as a number of other "movements" that need not be detailed here.

Finally, there was the political fact with which this book is concerned—the fall in voter participation. Table 5-1 addresses this development by partitioning the turnout differential between the end points of the period, 1960 and 1968. The following aspects of the table deserve comment.

Looking at the first section of the table, one notes that, just as for the full two-decade interval, the upward trend in socioeconomic status (primarily educational attainment) should have increased turnout over that of 1960, the base year. Looked at in probit terms, this increase was about 41 percent of the overall decline predicted by the model. Or, translating this into percentage terms (if nothing had changed except educational levels), turnout would have increased 1.2 percent, instead of decreasing 3.4 percent.

This upward pressure on turnout is, however, disproportionately less than that attributed to socioeconomic upgrading for the entire 1960–1968 period (3.9 percent). This means that the bulk of the effect from this upgrading, more than would be expected from the fact that twelve years are covered rather than eight, became operative in the later, 1968–1980 period. Inspection of Table 1-1, in which population proportions for characteristics were given, suggests that this is because a disproportionately small amount of the increase in educational attainment, as well as the shifts in occupational categories, occurred before 1968.

Moving down the table, two items stand out in the non-SES demographic characteristics section. The first is that the contribu-

Table 5-1

Explaining the Turnout Differential Between 1960 and 1968

variable	predicted decline	% of predicted decline	% of SES-adjusted decline
SOCIO-ECONOMIC CHARACTERISTICS			
education	-.047	-35.6	----
occupation, income	-.007	-5.3	----
all SES	-.054	-40.9	----
NON-SES DEMOGRAPHIC CHARACTERISTICS			
age	.014	10.7	7.6
marital status	.022	16.8	11.9
residential mobility	.011	8.4	5.9
race, region, sex	-.004	-3.1	-2.1
all non-SES demographic	.043	32.8	23.3
SOCIO-POLITICAL CHARACTERISTICS			
partisanship	.023	17.5	12.4
newspaper reading	.025	19.3	13.5
political efficacy	.094	71.3	50.8
all socio-political	.142	108.1	76.7
TOTAL PROBIT DROP	.131	100.0	100.0

percentage point decline in turnout predicted by probit model:　3.4
percentage point decline in turnout reported in ANES survey　:　3.4
percent of turnout differential explained by model　　　　　　:　100.0

tion of age to turnout decline is not nearly as large here as in the overall period. This is undoubtedly due to the fact that eighteen- to twenty-year-olds entered the electorate only *after* 1968. The second item worth noting is that the "all non-SES demographic" category accounts here for only about 33 percent of predicted probit decline (23 percent of adjusted), whereas, for the whole period, the same category accounts for about 63 percent (38 percent of adjusted). This suggests that, just as the upward push from socio-economic change was comparatively small in this period, so was the downward pressure from non-SES demographic change.

Not only were these changes—those from socioeconomic and non-SES demographic sources—similarly weak relative to later changes, they were of similar magnitude relative to one another. The former amounted (in magnitude) to 41 percent of decline, while the latter was about 33 percent. Thus, just as was seen when analyzing the 1960–1980 differential, the two forces roughly counterbalanced each other.

Looking now at the sociopolitical characteristics, one fact stands out dramatically. *The decline in political efficacy* is overwhelmingly the factor with the strongest impact on turnout levels. This single factor accounts for over 70 percent of predicted 1960–1968 turnout decline and over half the adjusted decline. By contrast, declining partisanship and newspaper reading account for only 18 percent and 19 percent, respectively, of predicted decline (12 percent and 14 percent of SES-adjusted decline). This means that the story of turnout decline in the 1960–1968 period is, to a great extent, the story of declining political efficacy.

This decline is political efficacy is not hard to understand, given the nature of the period. As will be recalled from earlier discussions, this efficacy variable taps people's feelings about whether their feelings and actions have much to do with what the government does (which, in turn, may be interpreted as an aspect of political alienation [Mason, House, and Martin 1981], although this controversy need not concern us here). One of the hallmarks of the 1960–1968 period was the emergence of movements and policy conflicts that produced the impression, on many people's parts, that the government was unresponsive to their wishes. This connection between the perception of increased distance between public policy and citizen preferences, on the one hand, and decreased political efficacy, on the other, has been well documented for the period (House and Mason 1975; Wright 1976) and makes sense in theoretical terms as well. This suggests that an historically based explanation for the decline in efficacy is appropriate (although alternative explanations will be considered later on in the chapter).

To summarize: socioeconomic upgrading in this period would have elevated turnout above its 1960 level (although not as much as later in the two-decade interval), thereby making the amount of turnout decline to be explained for the 1960–1968 period higher than the observed decline. Of this adjusted decline (right-hand column of Table 5-1), less than one-quarter can be accounted for by the shifting distribution of non-SES demographic characteristics (with a comparatively small contribution from the age category). The remainder of the decline—over three-quarters—can be attributed to sociopolitical change, with the overwhelming amount of that owing to the sharp drop in political efficacy.

The plausibility of this general story is enhanced by the figures at the bottom of the table. They show that the decrease in turnout predicted by the model is identical to that observed in the data. This shows that the variables in the model are doing a good job of predicting turnout levels, therefore making it less likely that there are important factors being left out of the story.

Additional Interpretation. The results presented in Table 5-1 may be further interpreted in the following manner. SES-upgrading made voting easier to handle for a substantial proportion of the population. The other demographic changes, however, made participation more difficult for many people. In terms of their effect on turnout, in fact, these forces were of similar magnitudes. Thus there was little net change in the extent to which the background characteristics of the population facilitated voting.

The effects of sociopolitical change, on the other hand, were all in the same direction. They uniformly decreased the extent to which the electorate found voting meaningful, chiefly through the sharp decline in political efficacy. The ease of voting, therefore, did not change much, but the extent to which the act seemed worthwhile to citizens did. Using the imagery of core and periphery, the demographic core and periphery remained about the same in size, while the political core shrank and its periphery expanded. It is worth noting that this is exactly the same pattern observed when analyzing the 1960–1980 turnout differential.

1968–1980. By 1972 the protest movements that emerged in the 1960s had died down considerably, and a new era in American politics had begun. Not that anyone claimed that faith in the system had replaced protest. Rather, a certain withdrawal from the political world seemed to occupy the space formerly held by social turbulence.

Several more concrete developments marked this new era, including, at least, (a) the profoundly disillusioning experience of

Watergate, (b) the dramatic transformation in campaign technologies, and (c) the extension of suffrage to eighteen- to twenty-year-olds. These were all developments of substantial importance. Finally, the post-1968 era was also an era of falling voter participation, just as the pre-1968 period was. This decline in turnout, from 1968 to 1980, is examined in Table 5-2, by partitioning the turnout differential between the end points of the period. The following items stand out most clearly in the table.

First, the upward push from socioeconomic upgrading (again, primarily educational attainment) is dramatic (93 percent of the

Table 5-2
Explaining the Turnout Differential Between 1968 and 1980

variable	predicted decline	% of predicted decline	% of SES-adjusted decline
SOCIO-ECONOMIC CHARACTERISTICS			
education	-.080	-66.1	----
occupation, income	-.032	-26.5	----
all SES	-.112	-92.6	----
NON-SES DEMOGRAPHIC CHARACTERISTICS			
age	.052	43.0	22.3
marital status	.023	19.0	9.9
residential mobility	.022	18.2	9.4
race, region, sex	.018	14.9	7.7
all non-SES demographic	.115	95.1	49.3
SOCIO-POLITICAL CHARACTERISTICS			
partisanship	.023	19.0	9.9
newspaper reading	.078	64.5	33.5
political efficacy	.017	14.0	7.3
all socio-political	.118	97.5	50.7
TOTAL PROBIT DROP	.121	100.0	100.0

percentage point decline in turnout predicted by probit model: 3.6
percentage point decline in turnout reported in ANES survey :   4.6
percent of turnout differential explained by model   : 78.3

magnitude of the decline in predicted probit, which translates into
2.9 points in percentage terms). This means that the amount of
turnout decline to be explained here is much larger than that observed in the data. Second, the downward push from non-SES demographic change is strong as well (about 95 percent of predicted
probit decline). Both of these changes are disproportionately greater
than they were in the 1960–1968 period. Also, the magnitude of
the two sets of changes is roughly equal, just as it was for 1960–
1968 and 1968–1980.

Among the non-SES social structural characteristics, age is easily the factor with the most influence on turnout levels, amounting
to 43 percent of predicted decline and 22 percent of the SES-adjusted total. The strong role played by age here, in contrast to its
weak role in the previous period, is clearly due to the extension of
voting rights to eighteen- to twenty-year-olds (see Table 1-1, 18–
24 age category after 1968).

Turning to the sociopolitical section of the table, the dominance
of one factor is again quite striking. The decline in newspaper
reading alone can be held responsible for almost two-thirds of net
turnout decline and about one-third of the SES-adjusted total. In
contrast, partisanship and political efficacy accounted for only 19
percent and 14 percent of decreased turnout, respectively (10 percent and 76 percent of the SES-adjusted figure). (It is interesting
to note here that almost all of the decline in political efficacy in
this era takes place between 1972 and 1976 [see Table 1-1], precisely the period during which the Watergate scandal made its impact on the American public.)

Thus *the decline in newspaper reading* is the crucial development during this period. As suggested earlier, following the campaign in the papers can best be interpreted as an indicator of campaign involvement and the stake in the electoral outcome that such
involvement fosters. Thus people read the papers less, were less
involved, and voted less. This shift in media consumption habits
could have had several causes.

One cause could have been changes in campaign technologies.
This change, described in detail by many authors (Blumenthal 1980;
Sabato 1981; Chagall 1981), chiefly consisted of television becoming the dominant form of political communication during campaigns. This did not mean, however, that people necessarily watched

more television programs concerning campaigns after 1968. In fact, this kind of television watching remained relatively stable (Shaffer 1981). What did change—indeed must have changed, given what we know of the extent to which the American public watches television—was the absorption of political information through this medium. The average citizen could not help absorbing dozens, even hundreds, of political television commercials during an election campaign (especially a presidential one). The result of this may have been that many citizens ceased following the campaigns in the papers, since so much "information" was available so cheaply through the everyday process of watching television, or because the constant repetition of political messages simply made them sick of politics.

Another possible cause for this decline in campaign newspaper reading could have been a generalized withdrawal from politics— a feeling that electoral political action was simply not worth even a minimal amount of personal effort. Given that such a withdrawal took place, one symptom of it may well have been not bothering to follow the campaign in the papers. Such a commitment to the election may have been viewed as too much trouble. This explanation for declining newspaper reading, as well as the one previously advanced, make sense in light of the period's history and suggest that such historically based explanations may be appropriate in this context (alternative explanations will be considered later in the chapter).

To summarize: socioeconomic upgrading (primarily educational) in this period would have elevated turnout considerably above its 1968 level if all other factors had remained unchanged, thereby making the amount of turnout decline to be explained larger than initially assumed. Of this SES-adjusted decline (right-hand column of Table 5-2), about half can be accounted for by the shifting distribution of demographic characteristics—especially that of age, owing to the suffrage extension for eighteen- to twenty-year-olds. The other half can be attributed to sociopolitical change, with the overwhelming proportion of that traceable to the sharp drop in campaign involvement through the newspapers.

The bottom part of Table 5-2 provides some evidence for the plausibility of this general story. This part of the table shows the match between predicted and observed decline (3.6 percent/4.6

percent). The match is close enough (predicted is 78 percent of observed) to suggest that the explanation advanced here is a good one. It is far enough off (22 percent), however, to indicate that there may be other factors depressing turnout in the 1968–1980 period that are not accounted for by the model. This possibility is given some added weight by the results of the interactive model, which estimated large period effects for 1972 and 1976, suggesting that unknown factors may have been operating in those two elections. Although the comparison here is with 1980, it is possible that such factors, if they existed in the latter two years, may have operated in this year as well (perhaps in a milder form). This possibility should be kept in mind when considering the results presented here.

Additional Interpretation. The results presented in Table 5-2 follow a familiar pattern. As previously, we have a situation in which voting was made easier for many people (SES-upgrading) but became harder for many as well (other demographic change, especially the addition of eighteen- to twenty-year-olds to the electorate). The result was, again, a standoff, in terms of the relationship between the population's background characteristics and the relative difficulty of participating. And exactly as previously, the effects of changes in political factors, here mostly the drop in campaign newspaper reading, were all in the same direction. Therefore, the ease of voting didn't markedly change, while the political dimensions of the act did. In core-periphery terms, the demographic periphery experienced little net change, while the political periphery expanded enormously.

Overall Summary. The interpretation offered above provides a convenient way of summarizing the findings of this section. Although the form of the story changed in the two periods, its essence remained the same. With regard to form, for instance, both the upward push from socioeconomic upgrading and the downward push from other demographic sources were found to be stronger in the later period than in the earlier one.

But in terms of essence, the result in both periods was remarkably similar: little change in the basic abilities/resources with which the electorate could handle the tasks of voting (the size of the demographic core of the electorate). This meant that the real change lay in the expansion of the political periphery of the system. Thus, although this expansion was for different reasons in different periods—declining belief in political effectiveness being dominant between 1960 and 1968 and declining campaign involvement being of prime importance between 1968 and 1980—the underlying story remained the same. Americans became disconnected from the political world, thereby found elections and their outcomes less meaningful, and, as a result, turnout rates went down.

The exposition in this section also included historically based explanations for the downward trends in political efficacy and campaign newspaper reading, trends that have played key roles in the analysis of turnout decline thus far. The 1960–1968 decline in efficacy was attributed to increased alienation or distance from government policies, while the 1968–1980 decline in newspaper reading was linked to the evolution of new campaign technologies and generalized withdrawal from politics (no explanation was offered, however, for the decline in partisanship). Although these explanations have strong bases in the historical events of those two decades, and hence have much to recommend them, there are alternative explanations that should be considered. This brings us to the subject matter of the next section.

Alternative Explanations for Sociopolitical Change

Demographic Position and Sociopolitical Change. The first explanation to be considered here is rooted in the well-established fact that an individual's demographic position generally bears a relationship to his or her set of political attitudes or behavior. So far, we have only considered the relationship between demographic position and one particular political behavior, voting. But it is reasonable to assume that social structure also bears a relationship to the other political variables that we have been concerned with: partisanship, political efficacy, and campaign newspaper reading. Given this, it is possible that, although social structural change could not directly account for turnout decline, it might nevertheless be responsible for it indirectly, through its effect on these three political variables. This possibility is investigated below.

The basic methodology to be used in this and other parts of the current section is similar to that used in previous chapters. Just as before, I will attempt to explain the shifts over time in the means of my dependent variables by changes over time in the distribution and/or effects of the independent variables in my model. This time my dependent variables are newspaper reading, political efficacy, and partisanship, rather than voting, and the regression technique used is ordinary least squares (OLS), rather than probit, since I am dealing with three point scales,[1] instead of a 0,1 dichotomous dependent variable. The fundamental idea is the same, however: to see how much of the distributional change over time in these variables can be attributed to changes in relevant predictors and how much must be attributed, in the final analysis, to "period effects" (i.e., effects of the historical period that have not been captured by the particular independent variables in the model).

Table 5-3 displays the first results from this phase of the investigation. For each of the three variables, three rows of coefficients are given. The first row gives the "gross" period effects for the variable—that is, the OLS coefficients for a regression that simply fits the five time dummies (1964, 1968, 1972, 1976, 1980) needed to represent the six elections covered by the pooled data, without any other independent variables in the equation. This simply fits the differences, over time, in the means of the dependent variables. The second row gives the "net" period effects for a regression model, including education (measured as previously). Education was added in first, and separately, because it trended in the opposite direction, relative to effect on turnout, than other demographic variables, and therefore might behave the same way in this context. The last row gives the net period effects from a regression that includes education, plus age, plus, of the remaining demographic variables, those with a significant relationship to the dependent variable in question. Categorizations used for the independent variables are congruent with those introduced in earlier chapters.

The theory behind this procedure is simple. If demographic distributional change is indeed implicated in the change over time of political efficacy, newspaper reading, and/or partisanship, the net period effects (rows two and/or three) should be considerably smaller than the gross effects (row one) displayed for the variable in question. Here this is quite obviously not the case. In no case are the period effects seriously attenuated by the addition of demographic

Table 5-3
Demographic Position and Sociopolitical Change: Coefficients of Time
Dummies in Different Models

	1964	1968	1972	1976	1980
CAMPAIGN NEWSPAPER READING					
time dummies only	-.029	-.089*	-.410*	-.227*	-.382*
+education	-.051	-.137*	-.472*	-.320*	-.504*
+age+marital status+sex +race+occupation+income	-.038	-.123*	-.423*	-.262*	-.445*
POLITICAL EFFICACY					
time dummies only	-.142*	-.365*	-.340*	-.458*	-.437*
+education	-.167*	-.417*	-.409*	-.563*	-.514*
+age+region+income	-.178*	-.428*	-.416*	-.560*	-.570*
PARTISANSHIP					
time dummies only	.070*	-.036	-.117*	-.146*	-.108*
+education	.072*	-.035	-.115*	-.143*	-.105*
+age+mobility+region+race +occupation+income	.077*	-.041	-.104*	-.131*	-.100*

* = coefficient is at least twice its standard error

Note: The third model adds the age variable, in each case, but other
demographic variables only where significant.

predictors to the regression model. For newspaper reading and efficacy, in fact, these effects are considerably larger in magnitude, once the demographic variables are added, than they were without any of these variables in the equation.

Comparisons of row two with row one for these two variables reveal that these increases in period effects are attributable to increased educational attainment over the twenty-year period. In other words, all other things being equal, rising educational levels should have considerably increased the levels of political efficacy and newspaper reading. This means, therefore, that the amount of decline that must be attributed to "history" becomes larger, and hence the magnitude of the period effects increases. (This is the same type of phenomenon discovered when looking at the turnout question itself, where there was an *actual* [i.e., observed] decrease in turnout and an "SES-adjusted" decrease that was considerably larger.) And, as can be seen from comparing the second and third rows, the rest of the demographic predictors do not seriously attenuate these education-adjusted period effects, so that the net result of demographic distributional change is to actually increase the magnitude of the drops in newspaper reading and efficacy that need to be explained.

As for partisanship, neither education alone nor in tandem with other demographic predictors is able to explain much of the change in this variable over the twenty-year time period. In fact, the impact here is almost nonexistent, either positively or negatively. Clearly, then, the changing distribution of individuals into various demographic positions is not a useful explanation for falling levels of either newspaper reading, political efficacy, or partisanship in the twenty-year time period.

A Cohort Phenomenon? The preceding subsection has explored the role of demographic attributes in turnout-relevant sociopolitical change. The negative results do not rule out another possibility that is worth considering. I am referring here to the entrance of new cohorts into the electorate and the role this may have played in causing these changes. "Cohort effects" have a long history in the study of voting behavior (Campbell et al. 1960; Converse 1976; Nie et al. 1976) and have been found to be of salience to a wide variety of electoral phenomena. These effects are theoretically grounded in the idea that groups entering the voting pool at the same time share certain formative experiences that cause them to react to the electoral universe in a similar manner.

A first indication of the possible role of cohorts in sociopolitical change may be gleaned from Tables 5-4, 5-5, and 5-6. These tables (Glenn 1977), one for each of the three variables under consideration, put individual cohorts on the rows, rather than age groups, as in standard cohort tables. This facilitates easy comparison both within and between cohorts. A preliminary examination by eye of these tables reveals a somewhat mixed pattern. To begin with, none of the tables displays the kind of stability on the horizontal that would suggest strong cohort effects—that is, where the mean level of a characteristic for a given cohort is set on entrance into the (voting) population and remains stable thereafter (from which it follows directly that a decline, for instance, in the level of that characteristic in the general population must be traceable to lower mean levels for entering cohorts). There are considerable indications that much of the variation in the tables must be attributed to the influence of period on all cohorts (or ages). For instance, looking at the newspaper reading table (Table 5-4), it is apparent that the massive drop in levels of this characteristic between 1968 and 1972 sweeps across all cohorts (between .2 and .4 in most cases) and is difficult to ascribe to entering cohorts particularly uninclined to use the print media.

With all that, however, close scrutiny of the tables reveals some suggestive patterns in the data. To return to the example just used, entering cohorts (i.e., those cohorts who have actually entered the electorate in the 1960–1980 time period) do seem to have levels of newspaper reading that are unusually low, even when con-

Table 5-4
COHORT TABLE I: Campaign Newspaper Reading

cohort	1960	1964	1968	1972	1976	1980
81+ in 1960	1.00					
77–80 in 1960	1.41	1.50				
73–76 in 1960	1.03	1.27	1.00			
69–72 in 1960	1.35	1.36	1.28	.90		
65–68 in 1960	1.38	1.33	1.38	.81	.98	
61–64 in 1960	1.51	1.35	1.12	1.00	1.12	.91
57–60 in 1960	1.47	1.33	1.35	1.16	1.03	1.18
53–56 in 1960	1.27	1.32	1.31	1.16	1.31	1.26
49–52 in 1960	1.38	1.43	1.25	1.16	1.26	1.00
45–48 in 1960	1.52	1.29	1.34	.91	1.13	1.14
41–44 in 1960	1.37	1.25	1.30	1.19	1.24	.96
37–40 in 1960	1.33	1.43	1.32	.96	1.17	.99
33–36 in 1960	1.37	1.30	1.35	.97	1.23	1.12
29–32 in 1960	1.40	1.35	1.37	1.08	1.25	1.22
25–28 in 1960	1.25	1.44	1.32	1.05	1.38	1.15
21–24 in 1960	1.25	1.23	1.22	.90	1.22	1.17
21–24 in 1964		1.14	1.10	.87	1.22	1.19
21–24 in 1968			1.05	.89	1.01	.90
21–24 in 1972				.71	1.01	.94
18–20 in 1972				.55	1.07	.72
18–21 in 1976					.76	.67
18–21 in 1980						.71
total	1.36	1.33	1.27	.94	1.13	.97

scale: 0 = no articles read
        1 = some articles read
        2 = many articles read

Table 5-5
COHORT TABLE II: Political Efficacy

cohort	1960	1964	1968	1972	1976	1980
81+ in 1960	1.24					
77-80 in 1960	.96					
73-76 in 1960	.95	1.17				
69-72 in 1960	1.29	1.08	.65	.86		
65-68 in 1960	1.40	1.05	.72	.78	.76	
61-64 in 1960	1.44	1.05	.94	.97	.74	.63
57-60 in 1960	1.39	.92	.90	.80	.47	.75
53-56 in 1960	1.45	1.12	.74	.84	.91	.92
49-52 in 1960	1.41	1.37	.86	.96	.98	.86
45-48 in 1960	1.56	1.24	.86	1.00	.89	.94
41-44 in 1960	1.52	1.34	1.04	1.04	1.08	.96
37-40 in 1960	1.52	1.38	1.16	1.15	.96	.98
33-36 in 1960	1.63	1.32	1.20	1.27	1.15	1.18
29-32 in 1960	1.54	1.47	1.26	1.26	1.19	1.27
25-28 in 1960	1.40	1.40	1.20	1.27	1.17	.91
21-24 in 1960	1.63	1.47	1.26	1.06	1.06	1.11
21-24 in 1964		1.49	1.20	1.22	1.09	1.09
21-24 in 1968			1.29	1.17	.96	1.06
21-24 in 1972				1.26	1.01	1.02
18-20 in 1972				1.23	1.02	1.07
18-21 in 1976					1.02	1.04
18-21 in 1980						1.01
total	1.46	1.32	1.09	1.12	1.00	1.02

scale: 0 = low efficacy
       1 = medium efficacy
       2 = high efficacy

sidered in the light of the population-wide post-1968 decline noted above. Such a pattern is even more noticeable in the partisanship table, where the lower levels of the characteristic seem concentrated in the part of the table where the entering cohorts are located (bottom right-hand side). Moreover, the horizontals in the table evidence more stability than in the other tables, further implicating cohort effects in the time trends for this variable (although it is also true that there is much less change to be accounted for here).

The political efficacy table, on the other hand, evidences little of the cohort-type pattern observed for newspaper reading and partisanship. The decline in this trait seems quite uniform across cohorts. Examination by eye of these three tables, then, would

Table 5-6
COHORT TABLE III: Partisanship

cohort	1960	1964	1968	1972	1976	1980
81+ in 1960	1.52					
77-80 in 1960	1.59	1.11				
73-76 in 1960	1.48	1.42	1.23			
69-72 in 1960	1.27	1.49	1.40	1.38		
65-68 in 1960	1.24	1.51	1.32	1.08	1.24	
61-64 in 1960	1.29	1.23	1.27	1.20	1.35	1.28
57-60 in 1960	1.33	1.37	1.31	1.29	1.23	1.29
53-56 in 1960	1.11	1.52	1.38	1.18	1.31	1.33
49-52 in 1960	1.20	1.32	1.28	1.35	1.10	1.41
45-48 in 1960	1.30	1.28	1.25	1.22	1.19	1.23
41-44 in 1960	1.19	1.32	1.10	1.15	1.14	1.25
37-40 in 1960	1.04	1.19	1.15	1.17	1.16	1.22
33-36 in 1960	1.24	1.22	1.09	1.22	1.23	1.16
29-32 in 1960	1.11	1.23	1.23	1.14	1.14	1.24
25-28 in 1960	1.14	1.18	1.15	1.00	1.05	1.18
21-24 in 1960	1.00	1.15	1.16	.99	.98	1.14
21-24 in 1964		1.15	.97	.94	.92	1.02
21-24 in 1968			.91	.91	.95	1.02
21-24 in 1972				.92	.89	.98
18-20 in 1972				.89	.91	.93
18-21 in 1976					.91	.88
18-21 in 1980						.89
total	1.24	1.29	1.18	1.11	1.07	1.12

scale: 0 = independent, apolitical
1 = weak partisan, independent leaner
2 = strong partisan

suggest the following ranking, in terms of likelihood of having significant cohort effects: (1) partisanship, (2) newspaper reading, and (3) political efficacy.

This hypothesized ranking—as well as the general hypothesis that there are, in fact, cohort effects operating here—can be subjected to an empirical test by regressing the three attitudinal variables on the demographic predictors used previously (see Table 5-3) plus period dummies *plus* a dummy variable for membership in a cohort that entered the electorate after 1956 (i.e., in one of the elections between 1960 and 1980). If cohort effects are indeed operative in the decline of these attitudinal traits, this cohort dummy should seriously attenuate the period effects observed in the previous regressions.[2]

The results of this procedure are shown in Table 5-7. The first row for each variable gives the period effects of the model that just includes the demographic predictors (exactly the same as the data given in row three for each variable in Table 5-3). The second row shows the period effects in an equation where the cohort dummy has been added. The results bear out the ranking alluded to above. Relatively little of the year-to-year change in efficacy can be attributed to cohort effects. As can be seen, the period effects are only slightly attenuated by the addition of the cohort dummy to the model. By contrast, the period effects for newspaper reading decline quite noticeably when this dummy is added—particularly after 1968. Even more impressive, the addition of the cohort variable to the partisanship regression cuts the period effects for 1972 and 1976 by about 38 percent, and the 1980 effect by 60 percent (again, though, there is less change to be accounted for on this variable).

These results are consistent with what is generally known about sociopolitical behavior in this and other periods. The strong impact of cohort on partisanship gibes well with previous scholarly

Table 5-7
Cohort and Sociopolitical Change: Coefficients of Time Dummies in Different Models

	1964	1968	1972	1976	1980
CAMPAIGN NEWSPAPER READING					
time dummies+education+age+ marital status+sex+race+occupation+income	-.038	-.123*	-.423*	-.262*	-.445*
+cohort dummy	-.027	-.102*	-.397*	-.223*	-.402*
POLITICAL EFFICACY					
time dummies+education+age+ region+income	-.177*	-.425*	-.415*	-.560*	-.570*
+cohort dummy	-.175*	-.422*	-.409*	-.549*	-.558*
PARTISANSHIP					
time dummies+education+age+ mobility+region+race+occupation+income	.077*	-.041	-.104*	-.131*	-.100*
+cohort dummy	.091*	-.014	-.065*	-.081*	-.040

* = coefficient is at least twice its standard error

findings about the relative stability of partisanship, once formed through initial political experiences (Converse 1976), and the declining level of partisanship among the new entrants to the political system (Nie et al. 1976). The role of cohorts in declining newspaper reading also makes sense, given what is known about media habit socialization at relatively young ages ("the television generation," etc.). Finally, the minor impact of cohort on political efficacy closely parallels the findings of House and Mason (1975) on increasing alienation (of which decreasing political efficacy was their most prominent example) across all U.S. population sectors in this time period.

Despite the new information gleaned from looking at cohort effects, however, it is still the case that the alternative explanations being considered in this section have not, thus far, adequately accounted for the decline in these sociopolitical characteristics over time. A glance at the first row in Table 5-3 for each of these characteristics (the gross effects of period without controlling for any other variables) and the corresponding final row in Table 5-7 (the period effects with education, age, significant other demographic variables, as well as cohorts, controlled for) makes this quite clear. Most of the secular decline in these traits remains to be explained—especially for newspaper reading and political efficacy. In fact, for these latter two variables, the period effects, in most cases, are still larger in magnitude at the end of this phase of analysis than they were at the beginning (again, this is because the education-adjusted decreases in the levels of these characteristics are considerably higher than the actual decreases).

Other Alternatives. Consideration of further possibilities is in order then. One such alternative may be derived from the structural logic of the investigation. It has been assumed that the direction of causation runs from sociopolitical characteristics to voting. Thus the decreases in the levels of certain sociopolitical characteristics are seen as being causal factors in the decline of turnout. It is within the realm of possibility that the direction of causation may run the other way: that the decline in voting levels has caused the decline in the levels of these characteristics. Although this is contrary to the theoretical framework within which this analysis is embedded—that, in fact, these characteristics both reflect and affect the meaningfulness of elections to voters, and thus *do* bear a causal relationship to turnout—the possibility is still plausible enough to deserve consideration.

There are two good reasons for supposing that this possibility does not accurately characterize the direction of causality. The first is the inadequacy of this viewpoint from the standpoint of temporal sequencing. The fact is that efficacy, partisanship, and newspaper reading *precede* in time the actual act of voting. In such an instance it is usually more reasonable to suppose that the event that precedes another in time is the causal agent, rather than the other way around, in the absence of compelling theoretical reasons for supposing the latter is the case.

Second, this view that the act of voting—or not voting—"causes" people's political characteristics does not receive empirical support where that view can be tested. For instance, if the decrease in voting has caused the decline in political efficacy, we would expect that the relationship between efficacy and turnout among respondents would be strengthened when those respondents actually go through the voting process. Thus, when the efficacy questions are asked *post*election, as opposed to *pre*election, the measured relationship between turnout and efficacy should be stronger. This does not turn out to be the case. For example, in 1960 the questions were asked preelection, whereas in 1968 and 1980 they were asked postelection. In all cases, however, the effect of efficacy was estimated to be the same. Even more tellingly, in 1972, a sample of the respondents were asked the efficacy questions both before and after the election. Their level of efficacy actually went up slightly, suggesting that the act of not voting can hardly be the causal agent in the decline of efficacy. In addition, a similar comparison produced negative results for the partisanship variable. Such a comparison could not be made for the newspaper reading variable.

A final reason for doubting the causal nature of voting, in this context, lies in the patterning evidenced by the decreases in efficacy and newspaper reading. If not voting was really the causal agent producing these decreases, one would not expect the patterning of the decreases to be so irregular. The steady decline in voting should have produced more or less steady declines in newspaper reading and efficacy. But, as discussed in the previous section, the changes in the sociopolitical characteristics have been quite episodic. Most of the decline in political efficacy, for instance, took place before 1968. Similarly, the preponderance of the fall in campaign newspaper reading took place after 1968. This does not suggest a causal logic that runs from not voting to feeling inefficacious and not reading the papers.

Another possibility is that decreases in efficacy, partisanship, and/or newspaper reading may have been caused by changes in other sociopolitical characteristics. It might be the case, for instance, that the decline in newspaper reading is simply a manifestation of the decline in campaign interest, or that the decline in partisanship reflects citizen's judgments that there is less difference between the political parties.

These possibilities are addressed by the data in Table 5-8. The table shows population proportions for campaign interest and perceived differences between the parties. The pattern of distributional change traced suggests that neither of the possibilities just alluded to are plausible ones. The level of campaign interest is only slightly lower in 1980 than in 1960. And the proportion who saw important differences between the parties was actually higher in the later year than in the earlier one. This makes it unlikely that the change in campaign interest caused the decline in campaign newspaper reading, or that the change in the perceived differences between the parties caused the decline in partisanship.

A final possibility concerns the campaign newspaper reading variable. One way of looking at this variable would interpret it purely as an indicator of the *expectation* to vote, which has a high correlation with actually voting. That is, people who expect to vote read the newspapers as preparation for voting, and this is the real significance of the campaign newspaper reading variable. Inspection of descriptive statistics, however, reveals that *levels of newspaper reading dropped as much for those expecting to vote as for those who didn't.* This suggests that campaign newspaper reading cannot be reduced to the expectation of voting, and, certainly, that the *decline* in the levels of newspaper reading has significance independent from trends in voting expectation.

As an additional check, some OLS regressions were run—results not shown—that regressed the three sociopolitical variables on various other sociopolitical characteristics with which they might plausibly be linked. Newspaper reading, for example, was regressed on partisanship and efficacy, as well as campaign interest

Table 5-8
Population Proportions for Campaign Interest and Differences Between Parties

	1960	1964	1968	1972	1976	1980
CAMPAIGN INTEREST						
interested	.770	.758	.805	.739	.804	.762
not interested	.230	.242	.195	.261	.196	.238
DIFFERENCES BETWEEN PARTIES						
important differences	.501	.592	.505	.459	.470	.579
not important differences	.499	.408	.495	.541	.530	.421

unweighted N = 8289

campaign interest based on responses to question:

Some people don't pay much attention to the political campaigns. How about you, would you say that you have been very much interested, somewhat interested, or not much interested in following the political campaigns so far this year?

differences between parties based on responses to question:

Do you think there are any important differences in what the Republicans and the Democrats stand for?

and expecting to vote. The results of this and other regressions did not indicate a significant role for characteristics of this nature in the decline of political efficacy, campaign newspaper reading, or partisanship.

One remark should be made before the findings on the origins of sociopolitical change are summarized. The first is that, although this discussion has been couched in terms of distributional changes—demographic, cohort, sociopolitical—the possibility was also investigated that changes over time in the effect of variables (i.e., interaction effects) could conceivably be responsible for the declining levels of the characteristics in question. This investigation added little of significance to the empirical findings discussed above, and hence is not detailed in the text. It does, however, underscore the manner in which sociopolitical change—especially decreasing efficacy and campaign involvement through the papers—has been fairly evenly distributed across the population.

Summary. This section has tested alternative explanations for the secular decreases in newspaper reading, political efficacy, and partisanship—characteristics tapping the three key sociopolitical trends implicated in turnout decline. This was done through examining the relationship of these characteristics to demographic position, cohort, and linked sociopolitical traits, as well as through examining the possibility that turnout is antecedent to these characteristics, rather than the other way around, as assumed. Demographic position was found to explain little of the decline for any of the variables, with two of the variables—efficacy and newspaper reading—actually exhibiting enhanced period effects, since the upward push of increased educational attainment was so strong.

Cohort was also unable to provide an explanation for the decreases on these two variables (particularly for efficacy), but did appear to be of substantial relevance to declining partisanship. Finally, attitudinal traits were found to be of little relevance.

This phase of the investigation has therefore shown that the origins of sociopolitical change relevant to turnout decline cannot be explained through variables logically suggested by the structure of the current model. The implication is that this change must therefore be traceable to sources exogenous to the model, to "history" if you will. This finding is consistent with the analyses advanced in the first part of this chapter, thereby enhancing the plausibility of the historically based explanations developed there.

Conclusion

The analyses performed in this chapter suggest the following interpretation of the decline in turnout in the United States between 1960 and 1980. In the initial phase of this period, 1960–1968, there was an upward push on turnout levels from socioeconomic upgrading, which was more than countered by (a) a precipitous drop in political efficacy, attributable to increased citizen alienation from government policy; and (b) more moderate distributional changes in several other turnout-related characteristics—

partisanship, marital status, etc. The net result was the observed fall in turnout over the eight-year period.

The second phase of the period, 1968–1980, was marked by an even stronger upward push on turnout levels from socioeconomic upgrading, meaning that the amount of turnout decline to be explained was substantially greater than it appeared to be at first glance—almost twice as large, in fact. This SES-adjusted decline was attributed to (a) the sharp decrease in campaign newspaper reading, viewed as a manifestation of changing campaign technologies and popular withdrawal from political concerns; (b) sudden growth in the younger end of the voter pool, owing to the entrance of eighteen- to twenty-year-olds into the electorate; and (c) other distributional changes of a less dramatic nature, including the post-Watergate fall in political efficacy, the continuing decline in partisanship—much of this apparently traceable to the entrance of newer cohorts into the voting pool—as well as increased residential mobility, and other demographic changes. Together, these three influences account for most of the fall in turnout over this twelve-year period.

Despite the differences between the two periods, they were marked by an underlying unity, which may be expressed using core-periphery terminology. In both periods the demographic core of the electorate expanded and contracted in roughly equal amounts, this core, therefore, remaining about the same size. In contrast, the political periphery expanded enormously in both periods. This meant that the links of Americans to their political system steadily weakened over the two decades, and consequently, the extent to which they found elections to be meaningful events declined steadily as well. This is, on balance, the reason why the polling booths emptied out between 1960 and 1980.

This chapter has completed the task of identifying the proximate causes for declining turnout in the United States between 1960 and 1980. It is now appropriate to discuss the substantive importance of these findings.

Notes

1. Partisanship and efficacy were already constructed as three-point interval scales when used as independent variables. Examination of turnout

rates for the categories of the newspaper reading variable, as well as difference in goodness-of-fit tests for interval, as opposed to categorical, treatment of the variable, convinced me that newspaper reading could legitimately be made an interval scale when used as the dependent variable in regressions.

2. It is well known that using age, period, and cohort in the same regression can present identification problems, since any one of these variables is a re-expression of the information contained in the other two. In this case, however, the age variable does not exhaust the age information (i.e., is considerably simplified from the seventeen or more categories that could be used to summarize this information), and the cohort variable is only a single dummy, so having these variables in a regression, along with period, should not produce such problems.

6

The Changing American Nonvoter, 1960–1980

Frank J. Fahrenkopf Jr., the Republican national chairman, predicted today that the Republicans would beat the Democrats at registering new party members this year.

Mr. Fahrenkopf told the Republican National Committee at its preconvention meeting that his goal was to register two million new Republicans by Election Day and "at this point in time" more than 1.5 million had been registered.

—Item in *New York Times*, 8-17-84

The key findings presented thus far have been the following. First, there was a cluster of results concerning the influence of demographic change on turnout levels. It was determined that increased educational attainment—as well as an upgrading of the income and occupation distributions—acted to push turnout upward. (Americans became more "middle class.") But, at the same time, the proportions of the electorate that were young, residentially mobile, and single increased, acting to depress turnout levels. (Americans became less socially "rooted.") The effects of these two sets of changes were of the same magnitude, so the net impact of demographic change on turnout was negligible.

It was therefore determined that the crucial factors in reducing turnout levels lay in the political realm. Three factors were identified as being of salience: (1) decline in citizens' perception of their ability to influence government actions (decreased political efficacy); (2) decline in campaign involvement (decreased campaign newspaper reading); and (3) decline in partisanship (decreased party identification). These three trends were identified as part of a process of political disconnection or "peripheralization" that reduced the meaningfulness of electoral participation to Americans.

These two sets of changes involved in turnout decline—social structural and sociopolitical—each have substantive implications.

Implications of Structural Change

It has long been a popular view that the pool of American nonvoters is concentrated among the lowest socioeconomic segments of society. Burnham (1982) says "the 'party of non-voters' is concentrated among the poorest and most dependent social classes." He goes on to attribute the growth of this party to the failure of the system to meet the needs of the socioeconomically deprived, who join this party in ever larger numbers. Beliefs along these lines underpin most of the more extravagant claims for the political potential of mobilizing nonvoters. Because these potential voters are increasingly from the "lower class," and therefore, presumably, left of center, their mobilization would decisively change the complexion of American politics (Rogers 1984).

There are two problems with this view. First, because the sets of changes relevant to turnout levels include (a) socioeconomic upgrading, (b) other demographic changes not necessarily heavily grouped on socioeconomic categories (increased proportions young, mobile, single), and (c) political changes that made their impact felt across the population, there is no compelling reason to believe that the pool of nonvoters has become increasingly skewed toward the lowest socioeconomic categories. And, in fact, this does not appear to be the case (see Table 6-1). An elementary measure of disproportionality, for instance (ratio of proportion of nonvoting population in a given category to proportion of overall population in that category), for 1960 and 1980, reveals relatively little change over time (1.48 to 1.52 for high school dropouts; 1.39 to 1.26 for poor people).

What did happen between 1960 and 1980, as a result of the

Table 6-1

Comparing the American Nonvoter, 1960 and 1980: Proportions of
Voters and Nonvoters in Selected Population Categories

	1960 all	1960 voters	1960 non-voters	1980 all	1980 voters	1980 non-voters
EDUCATION						
0-12 years	.486	.424	.724	.257	.204	.390
12	.290	.322	.171	.354	.346	.375
13-15	.120	.132	.070	.211	.224	.179
16 or more	.104	.123	.035	.177	.225	.057
AGE						
18-24 years	.033	.023	.068	.145	.104	.246
25-28	.086	.074	.130	.103	.086	.146
29-32	.085	.076	.119	.088	.085	.094
33-36	.103	.111	.070	.088	.089	.087
37 or more	.694	.715	.612	.576	.636	.427
MARITAL STATUS						
not married-SP (1)	.198	.183	.255	.394	.353	.496
married-SP	.817	.802	.745	.606	.647	.504
RESIDENTIAL MOBILITY						
mobile within two years	.254	.225	.366	.332	.264	.501
not mobile	.746	.775	.634	.668	.736	.499
OCCUPATION						
housewives	.249	.218	.369	.160	.152	.179
blue collar (2)	.284	.280	.298	.237	.202	.323
white collar and other	.467	.502	.333	.603	.646	.499
FAMILY INCOME						
poor (3)	.434	.390	.604	.347	.311	.437
non-poor	.566	.610	.396	.653	.689	.563
PARTISANSHIP						
independent, apolitical	.126	.092	.255	.147	.100	.263
weak partisan, leaner	.512	.519	.482	.589	.585	.600
strong partisan	.363	.389	.263	.264	.315	.136
POLITICAL EFFICACY						
low efficacy	.153	.103	.344	.319	.257	.471
middle efficacy	.235	.221	.287	.340	.340	.340
high efficacy	.612	.676	.369	.341	.402	.189
CAMPAIGN NEWSPAPER READING						
no articles	.198	.135	.436	.290	.208	.491
some articles	.249	.238	.293	.447	.471	.387
many articles	.553	.627	.271	.263	.320	.122

(1), (2), (3) see explanations in Table 1-1.

trends detailed in this investigation, was a decrease in the extent to which nonvoters were concentrated—in an absolute sense—in the lowest socioeconomic categories. This is because there are proportionally fewer people in these categories—thus fewer nonvoters for socioeconomic reasons—*and* more people moving into the nonvoting pool for non-socioeconomic reasons. The net result of these two trends was a substantial shift in the profile of the American nonvoter.

The data in Table 6-1 illustrate this shift. While in 1960, 72 percent of nonvoters had less than a high school education, by 1980 this figure had dropped to only 39 percent. Similarly, in 1960, 60 percent of nonvoters were poor, whereas only 44 percent were in 1980. On the other side of the coin, about 7 percent of nonvoters were under age twenty-five in 1960, whereas 25 percent were in 1980. Or, 37 percent and 26 percent were mobile and single, respectively, in 1960, but by 1980 each of these categories captured half of the nonvoting population.

Thus, although in 1960 it might have been quite reasonable to describe the American nonvoter as a poor high school dropout, this description is no longer so compelling in 1980. The pool of nonvoters is much more dispersed among socioeconomic categories, and other categories as well. Nonvoters, then, cannot be easily typecast as residing on the absolute lowest rungs of the social structure.

Nor, as mentioned earlier, has their relative representation among the lowest socioeconomic categories changed much. But it is still the case that there *are* skews, socioeconomic and otherwise, in the distribution of nonvoters. That is, nonvoters are not a faithful demographic representation of the general population, but are disproportionally concentrated in certain categories. From this viewpoint, it could be argued that, despite the failure of the nonvoting population to display an overwhelmingly depressed socioeconomic profile, these skews are strong enough to make a general mobilization of nonvoters politically dramatic (if no more dramatic than it might have been twenty years ago).

This is where the second problem comes in. Skews in partisan bias and political views by demographic category are not strong enough to make such a scenario plausible. Wolfinger and Rosenstone (1980, pp. 80–88) estimate, for instance, that a general increase of 9 percent in the turnout rate would only produce a .3 percent increase in Democratic sympathies. This finding does not reflect the fact that there are no demographic skews, or no partisan skews by demography, but rather that the combined impact of these skews is not large enough to make a big difference when the number of voters is simply increased at random by drawing from the nonvoting population.

Thus the view that the contemporary pool of nonvoters is increasingly huddled at the bottom of the social structure, ready to transform the nature of American politics in a predetermined direction, is shown to be of questionable plausibility. Instead, nonvoters are spread across demographic and partisan categories, and their political impact could therefore vary widely, depending on which *parts* of that population are mobilized into the electoral arena. In implicit recognition of these facts, (a) tendencies across the political spectrum are seeking to reach nonvoters through voter registration and other efforts—these potential voters are no longer seen as naturally belonging to the Democrats or the left (Perlez 1984); and (b) where these efforts are being pursued, they are of a *targeted* nature, seeking to reach subpopulations of nonvoters whose probability of voting "right" is greater—and, it is hoped, overwhelmingly greater (i.e., Democratic registration of blacks)— than the overall pool of abstentionists.

To put a finer point on it, when the advantages of higher turnout are alluded to, in partisan terms, it should always be kept in mind that such advantages are mostly dependent on which *part* of the nonvoting pool is under consideration. It makes perfect sense to contend, for instance, that higher mobilization of a population group that votes 60 percent Democratic will benefit the Democrats. It makes less sense to insist that high turnout per se will automatically benefit the Democrats, or that high turnout is necessarily the "key" to any given election. After all, to mobilize more of a population group that votes 60 percent Democratic presupposes that one *has* a population group that votes 60 percent Democratic. As recent history attests (witness the decline in union member support for the Democrats), these groups can be hard to come by. The turnout "key" thus becomes inseparably linked with the general political problem of reaching the groups most likely to be one's supporters among the electorate.

Implications of Political Change

The implications of the political changes relevant to turnout decline—the generalized disconnection from the political world—may
be better understood by recalling an observation made earlier about
comparative differences in turnout rates. These differences, where
the U.S. turnout rate is generally far lower than that of other in-
dustrialized democracies, have been attributed to the facts that (a)
registration is state sponsored in these other countries, thereby
making it considerably easier for the individual citizen to qualify
to vote; and (b) political parties in these nations play a much
stronger role in commanding voter loyalty and mobilizing citizens
to go to the polls.

These comparative differences may be summed up by saying that
voting is, to a large extent, a collective responsibility in other democracies. The state and the political parties actively attempt to
engage citizens in the electoral process, thereby taking a considerable amount of the burden of voting off the shoulders of the individual. In contrast, in the United States, the state plays almost
no role, and the parties, comparatively little, in mobilizing the voter
into the electoral arena. It is the individual responsibility of the
voter to register, find out enough to differentiate between candidates, make a decision, and act to ratify that decision by casting
his or her ballot.

This observation may be related to the research findings in the
following manner. Let us recall that the two political factors most
important in explaining turnout decline were the decreases in political efficacy and campaign newspaper reading. One is an atti-
tude and the other is an activity, but they both tap important ways
that individuals interface with an election campaign. The first, political efficacy, expresses the extent to which an individual feels
that his or her individual actions have any effect on government
actions. The second, campaign newspaper reading, measures the
extent of an individual's campaign involvement through the medium of the papers.

Thus two critical ways in which individuals linked themselves
to the voting process changed. On the one hand, far fewer people
felt that their political actions—of which voting is the most common example—were effective in influencing the government. Thus

this crucial individual motivation to vote was undermined. On the other hand, people ceased taking the trouble to follow the campaign in the papers because of some combination of a changing media environment and general political withdrawal. This made the individual voter, whose responsibility it was to be informed about and involved in the campaign, less informed and involved, and thus less inclined to vote.

In a sense, voters were "dropping out" of politics at the individual level, both attitudinally and behaviorally. Their commitments, such as they were, to the political system were eroding. In a society like the United States, where voting is heavily dependent on individual responsibility and motivation, this naturally produced a decline in the voting rate. No collectivities stood willing (or perhaps even able) to pick up this slack in the electoral system and ensure turnout at the polls. Thus not only is the United States a society in which the turnout rate is traditionally low because of the lack of collectivities that organize the act of voting for citizens, but it is also a society whose *decline* in turnout rates is bound up with the system of individual responsibility for voting.

In one sense, this story may be looked at as good news. It does not appear that the decline in turnout is linked to some form of radical revulsion with democracy or contemporary society, but rather to the erosion of this individually focused system of voter participation. It was perhaps inevitable that this system should weaken under the press of historical events (as the findings in this investigation suggest that it has). But it hardly implies that this weakening could or will evolve to the point of political collapse.

In another sense, the story, if it does not qualify as bad news, certainly poses a thorny problem. How can the problem of low voter turnout be dealt with in the context of an individual system of electoral participation (not well designed for high voter turnout in the first place) that has been seriously weakened by social and political developments?

There are two possible ways this problem could be dealt with. The first way would be through revamping the individual system of voting responsibility, so that it works more like it did in the 1950s than in the 1970s. This could be done by somehow recreating the "system of the 1950s" (described in chapter 1) or by introducing a new individually oriented system of electoral participation that, although structured differently from the system of the 1950s, works as well in promoting turnout.

The second way the voter turnout problem could be addressed would be by replacing the individual system of voting responsibility with a collectively oriented one, such as most European countries have. This would entail a much more active role for the state and political parties in the United States in registering voters and mobilizing them to go to the polls.

Movement in the first direction seems more likely. However, even if there are changes that favor the individual system of electoral participation, there is the possibility that these changes might not really work. The individually oriented participation system is basically a weak one, and it is possible that it works (relatively) well only under certain historical conditions. If this is true, once the historical conditions have passed, the system may prove difficult to resuscitate or restructure.

Movement in the second direction, toward a collectively oriented system of electoral participation, although less likely to occur, would put voter turnout on a firmer foundation. Such a system would be relatively robust and provide an organized, ongoing way of getting voters to the polls. Precisely because of its organized and ongoing character, however, it requires more of a conscious social will to put in place.

It will be interesting to see in what direction the American system of electoral participation evolves—or whether it evolves at all—in the latter part of the twentieth century. Some clues about this may be found by examining the results from the 1984 presidential election, the first one held after the period of uninterrupted turnout decline between 1960 and 1980.

7

The American Nonvoter
Revisited: The 1984 Election

This chapter examines the 1984 election in light of the findings from the research on the 1960–1980 elections. The following topics are examined: (a) the partisan impact of turnout and turnout-related activities in the 1984 election; (b) an analysis of the difference in turnout levels between the 1984 and 1980 elections using the model previously developed; and (c) the implications of this analysis for the future of voter turnout in the United States.

Partisan Impact of Turnout in 1984

The 1984 election was marked by an enormous amount of activity around increasing voter turnout. Both political parties, and quite a number of issue groups, put considerable effort in getting more voters to the polls, chiefly through registering new voters. Particularly among the Democrats, the idea was that if a party put effort into registering new voters, that party would reap a significant partisan reward from the voters it helped bring to the polls.

The flaws in this line of reasoning were discussed in detail in the previous chapter. Because nonvoters do not differ much from voters in their political preferences and the demographic and partisan skews among them are not as severe as is generally supposed, it is actually a rather difficult project for a political party to benefit from simply adding more voters to the rolls.

And, indeed, this turned out to be the case in the 1984 election.

Although millions of new voters were registered—registration went up 3.2 percent over 1980 (Committee for the Study of the American Electorate, 1984)—the partisan results of this registration activity were trivial. Partially, this was because the registration activities of the Democratic party and allied organizations were offset by registration efforts of the Republicans and their allies.

More important, new voters acted politically like the rest of the population—only more so. They went two to one for Reagan (Osborne 1985), despite all the efforts of the Democratic party to find and register the poorest and most deprived sectors of the nonvoting population. This underscores how increased voter turnout is more likely to reinforce the results of an election than change them. Given this, the Democrats' hopes for their registration activities were clearly misplaced.

Analyzing the Turnout Differential Between 1980 and 1984

Although there was little of partisan importance about turnout in the 1984 election, there was something of general social and political significance. *For the first time in twenty-four years, turnout went up in a presidential election.* This reversed a twenty-year period of uninterrupted turnout decline.

That said, it should be emphasized that turnout did not go up very much. The increase in voter participation was only .7 percent (Osborne 1985), making a relatively small dent in the ten-point drop that turnout rates experienced between 1960 and 1980.

Still, although the change was small, the direction of the change was an important development. Did this increase in turnout portend a return to the "system of the 1950s," in which turnout levels were relatively high? Was American society rebounding from the trends that made Americans less socially rooted and less connected to their political system, and thus less likely to vote?

The data in Table 7-1, which shows the change in population proportions of turnout-related characteristics between 1980 and 1984, provide support for the idea that America was returning to the system of the 1950s. First, the trend toward a less socially rooted population was basically reversed. Although there was a decrease in the proportion married and living with spouse, which does continue the trend of the past twenty years, trends in age and residential mobility reversed themselves.

Instead of decreasing, the proportion of the population who had not moved within two years increased by a fairly substantial .04. And, reflecting the aging of the baby boom generation, the age profile of the population became older rather than younger. Population proportions of the three oldest age categories all went up, with the twenty-nine- to thirty-two-year-old group going up .015, the thirty-three- to thirty-six-year-old group up .02, and the thirty-seven + group up .009. Both age and residential mobility are among the strongest demographic predictors of voter turnout, so these trends are of special significance.

Even more significant, and especially suggestive of a return to the system of the 1950s, are the trends on the sociopolitical characteristics. All three variables show changes in the opposite direction from the previous twenty years.

Campaign newspaper reading generally increased, with the proportion reading at least some campaign articles in the newspaper going up .066. Partisanship went up significantly, with the strong partisanship category increasing by .036. And political efficacy showed a dramatic upward shift, as the high efficacy category increased by .155. Thus, between 1980 and 1984, Americans became more connected to the political system, at least in the ways that were of importance in the 1950s.

Finally, socioeconomic upgrading, described in detail in earlier chapters, continued between 1980 and 1984. Educational attainment, on balance, continued to rise. Although the proportion of college graduates did decline by .01, the proportion of high school graduates went up by .018 and the proportion with at least some college increased by .034. And, although the income distribution between poor and nonpoor did not change, the occupational distribution did experience an upward shift of .058 in the white collar and other category.

Thus it would appear that between 1980 and 1984, both the demographic and the political core expanded. In terms of the demographic core, the population became more socially rooted, as well as experiencing continued socioeconomic upgrading. And, in terms of the political core, there was a strengthening of several key links between Americans and their political system.

Table 7-1
Population Proportions of Turnout-Related Characteristics, 1980–1984

	1980	1984	Change
EDUCATION			
0-11 years	.258	.215	-.043
12	.354	.372	+.018
13-15	.211	.245	+.034
16 or more	.177	.167	-.01
AGE			
18-24 years	.145	.123	-.022
25-28	.103	.082	-.021
29-32	.088	.103	+.015
37 or more	.576	.585	+.009
MARITAL STATUS			
not married-SP (1)	.394	.422	+.028
married-SP	.606	.578	-.028
RESIDENTIAL MOBILITY			
mobile within 2 years	.332	.292	-.04
not mobile	.668	.708	+.04
OCCUPATION			
housewives	.160	.144	-.016
blue collar (2)	.237	.195	-.042
white collar and other	.603	.661	+.058
FAMILY INCOME			
poor (3)	.347	.347	0
non-poor	.653	.653	0
SEX			
female	.563	.560	-.003
male	.437	.440	+.003
RACE			
non-white	.161	.185	+.024
white	.839	.815	-.024
REGION			
south	.271	.241	-.03
non-south	.729	.759	+.03
PARTISANSHIP			
independent, apolitical	.147	.133	-.014
weak partisan, leaner	.589	.567	-.022
strong partisan	.264	.300	+.036
POLITICAL EFFICACY			
low efficacy	.319	.292	-.027
middle efficacy	.340	.212	-.128
high efficacy	.341	.496	+.155
CAMPAIGN NEWSPAPER READING			
no articles	.290	.232	-.058
some articles	.447	.513	+.066
many articles	.263	.255	-.008

(1), (2), (3) see explanations in Table 1-1.

In light of these developments, the idea that the system of the 1950s, with its relatively high voter turnout, was being re-created seems plausible. In fact, the puzzling thing is that it wasn't being re-created faster. Given the positive nature of the trends on almost all turnout-related characteristics, and the extensive voter registration activities, it is surprising that turnout went up only .7 percent.

Insight into this possible discrepancy between the factors favoring increased turnout and how much turnout actually went up may be gained by applying the model developed earlier to the 1984 data. The model will predict how much turnout should have gone up, given the changes in the population just described, which can then be compared with measured changes in turnout levels.

The results from the model are shown in Table 7-2. As with analogous tables in chapters 4 and 5, the change in turnout predicted by the model—expressed in probit terms—is parceled out among the various factors and sets of factors in the model (column one). Then, the relative contributions of different factors to turnout change is assessed in percentage terms (column two). Note that here a predicted increase rather than decrease is being analyzed, so that a positive number indicates a contribution to probit *increase*, rather than *decrease*, as was previously the case.

As was suggested by the discussion of the data in Table 7-1, the characteristics in each part of the table make a contribution to predicted turnout increase. The three components of socioeconomic status, education, occupation, and income, together account for .03, or 21.1 percent, of the predicted increase. Most of this comes from the increase in educational attainment.

Actually, the contribution of changes in SES characteristics to probit increase is not a new story, the same phenomenon having been observed in the analysis of the 1960–1980 data. What is new are the contributions of characteristics in the other two parts of the table.

Looking first at non-SES demographic characteristics, the combined impact of changes on these variables was to generate .03 in probit increase, 21.1 percent of the total predicted increase. This was basically due to an older and less residentially mobile voter pool, and stands in sharp contrast to the role of this cluster of variables between 1960 and 1980. In that period, changes in these demographic characteristics essentially canceled out the upward

Table 7-2

Explaining the Turnout Differential Between 1980 and 1984

variable	predicted increase	% of predicted increase
SOCIO-ECONOMIC CHARACTERISTICS		
education	.019	13.8
occupation, income	.01	7.3
all SES	.03	21.1
NON-SES DEMOGRAPHIC CHARACTERISTICS		
age	.013	9.2
marital status	-.006	-4.6
residential mobility	.017	12.0
race, region, sex	.006	4.4
all non-SES demographic	.03	21.1
SOCIO-POLITICAL CHARACTERISTICS		
partisanship	.019	13.6
newspaper reading	.017	11.8
political efficacy	.046	32.5
all socio-political	.081	57.8
TOTAL PROBIT INCREASE	.141	100.0

percentage point increase in turnout predicted by probit model: 4.1
percentage point increase in turnout reported in ANES survey: 2.3
percent of turnout differential explained by model   :   178.3

push on turnout from socioeconomic upgrading. In the 1980–1984 period, although still of the same magnitude, changes in these characteristics, particularly the ones tapping social "rootedness," also provided an upward push on turnout and reinforced the impact of socioeconomic upgrading.

Turning to the sociopolitical characteristics, the contrast with the 1960–1980 period is even more startling. Together, increases in partisanship, campaign newspaper reading, and political efficacy account for .081 or 57.8 percent of the predicted probit increase, with the largest contribution from enhanced political efficacy (by itself generating almost one-third of the predicted increase). Thus, instead of countering and in fact overwhelming the upward push on turnout from socioeconomic upgrading, as was the case between 1960 and 1980, changes in sociopolitical characteristics between 1980 and 1984 provided an *additional* upward push on turnout—*an upward push almost three times the magnitude of that from socioeconomic upgrading.*

The combined impact of all these changes was to generate a predicted probit increase of .141, a substantial figure that translates into a predicted turnout increase of 4.1 percent. Thus the question of whether there is a discrepancy between the factors that favored increased turnout, and how much turnout actually increased in 1984 may be answered in the affirmative. The model says that, given the extent of turnout-promoting changes in population characteristics, the increase in turnout should have been much higher than the .7 percent that obtained in the actual election, or even the 2.3 percent self-reported increase in the ANES data.

To what can this discrepancy be attributed? The best explanation is that there is another factor(s) operative at this point that is depressing turnout and holding down turnout increase in spite of the otherwise favorable conditions. This unknown factor is not included in the model, whereas all the factors that are currently promoting turnout are, thus producing the overoptimistic turnout increase prediction.

The idea that there is an unknown factor acting on turnout levels in this period is consistent with results from the 1960–1980 analysis. Although the model accounted perfectly for the drop in turnout between 1960 and 1968, it underpredicted the decrease for the 1968–1980 period. This suggests that, as in the 1980–1984 period just analyzed, there was another factor not in the model acting to depress turnout. It is a reasonable guess that this unknown turnout-depressing factor has been the same in both periods, although apparently its effects have become stronger over time, since the magnitude of the discrepancy between predicted and actual change has increased.

It is also possible that the same unknown factor acting to hold down turnout increase is responsible for the increased overreporting of turnout. That is, while actual turnout went up only .7 percent, self-reported turnout went up 2.3 percent. This indicates that more respondents than previously are saying that they voted when in fact they did not, producing the inflated turnout increase in the American National Election Studies (ANES) data. This may reflect a situation in which many people felt, because of the sociopolitical changes described earlier, more connected to the political system but somehow still not motivated enough to actually vote, owing to the unknown factor whose existence has been hypothesized. Such a contradictory situation could have significantly increased voter inclinations to misrepresent their participation in the election without doing much to actually get them into the polling booth. This scenario provides a plausible explanation for the different levels of turnout increase observed in the "real world" and reported by respondents in the ANES survey. And the root cause of this phenomenon would be the same as that responsible for slow turnout increase—an unknown turnout-depressing factor operating on the voting population.

Overall, these results strongly suggest that the "system of the 1950s" is *not* being re-created, despite trends in the distribution of turnout-related characteristics that suggested this might be the case. That system may have really only been appropriate for the particular historical conditions within which it arose, and simply will not work under contemporary conditions, even if social change appears to favor its revival. The implications of this will be discussed in more detail in the final section.

The results also suggest an interesting reformulation of the key research question around turnout. While before the 1984 election, attention was focused on solving the "puzzle of turnout decline"—why turnout declined in the face of social developments that should have produced increased voter turnout—attention should now shift to another puzzle, the "puzzle of slow turnout increase." The puzzle of slow turnout increase is why turnout has increased so slowly in the face of social and political developments that should have produced rapid turnout increase. Solving this puzzle entails identifying the unknown turnout-depressing factor (or factors) that has been acting as a counterforce to the turnout-promoting changes described in detail in this section. Successfully identifying this factor would be a notable achievement for turnout researchers and would undoubtedly shed more light on contemporary U.S. voter turnout than further attempts to analyze turnout decline in the 1960–1980 period.

Implications for Future of U.S. Voter Turnout

If the system of the 1950s is unlikely to be reinvigorated, as these findings indicate, it is important to ask why this is so. Without presuming to identify the unknown factor depressing turnout levels, which is the proximate cause of the difficulties in reviving the relatively high turnout rates of the 1950s, the following line of analysis provides some insight into how historical conditions may now be generally unsuitable for the system of that era.

One influential school of thought about American politics views American electoral history in terms of periodic phenomena known as "critical realignments" (Burnham 1970). These realignments took place in conjunction with turning point or critical elections, spaced at intervals of twenty-eight to thirty-six years: 1800, 1828, 1860, 1896, and 1932. Burnham characterizes them as being short-lived but intense disruptions of traditional voting patterns, where one-fifth to one-third of the electorate shift partisan allegiance, a dramatic portion of that shift taking place at the critical elections noted above. Elections in general during these realignments are marked by an unusual political intensity, as polarization within parties and issue distances between them increase significantly. The population as a whole evidences higher rates of political mobilization and participation. And the end result is a changed political landscape in which the nature and meaning of politics for the average voter has been redefined.

The last critical election was in 1932. The system of the 1950s really represented the stable period of the critical realignment initiated by that election. A politics whose nature and meaning had been defined by the critical realignment of the 1930s was the foundation of that system. This suggests that besides the sociopolitical characteristics whose role in connecting Americans to their political system has been described, there may have been another way (or ways) in which Americans were linked to the electoral system that derived its strength from the political definitions of the previous critical realignment. Such a link would have been on a more basic level than those of partisanship, efficacy, and campaign involvement and might have involved a certain acceptance of the political arrangements in society as meaningful and valid.

Whatever the precise nature of this link, it makes sense that the definitions undergirding the link would erode over time as chronological distance from the critical realignment increased. Now, under normal circumstances, another critical realignment would have taken place and replaced the weakened old political definitions with new ones. But the general consensus is that no such critical realignment has taken place since the 1950s. Instead, if anything, "dealignment" has taken place, whereby the loyalties of voters have become more amorphous and their ideologies cloudier.

Signs of dealignment became particularly strong after the election of 1968, which is thirty-six years after the critical election of 1932. Thus, at the very point at which the periodicity of American electoral history typically brings forth a critical realignment to replace old political definitions with new ones, dealignment took center stage instead. *And it is precisely in this period after the 1968 election that the model first suggests the presence of an unknown factor depressing turnout levels.* This timing supports the idea (although by no means proves) that the unknown factor depressing turnout levels is bound up with the decaying political definitions of the last critical realignment.

If this line of analysis is correct, it would explain why it has been so difficult to revive the system of the 1950s, despite social and political trends that appeared to be moving in that direction. The system of the 1950s was rooted in particular historical conditions that helped give it its relative strength as a promoter of turnout, but which have now changed significantly. This suggests that it is probably impossible to revive the system of the 1950s, even if it is possible to reproduce or approximate some of its features.

And this may be a fair way of summing up the developments since 1980. While changes in American politics under Reagan have apparently succeeded in strengthening some important connections of Americans to their political system, connections that were an important part of the system of the 1950s, it has proved impossible to reproduce the system itself because of the lack of more fundamental changes in American politics. Thus the upward swing in the American political mood since 1980 has produced a political culture with some similarity to that of the 1950s—certainly more so than has been the case for a number of years—but this similarity is chiefly on the surface, a shadow lacking substance, because of the altered historical conditions.

If the system of the 1950s cannot be revived, what is the likely future of American voter turnout? On one level, there is some cause for alarm. If all the voter registration activity and favorable social/political trends only succeeded in raising voter participation .7 percent, then it is possible that another decline in voter turnout could be in the offing. This would happen if the unknown turnout-depressing factor, whose origins have been speculated about, continued to exert as strong a downward pressure on turnout levels, while registration activities, and particularly the influence of the favorable trends, declined.

Whether this happens or not, it does illustrate how precarious the current situation with voter turnout is. Within the context of present political arrangements, there appears to be little reason to expect substantial turnout increases and some reason for fearing further decreases.

There are two ways this situation could change. The first way would be if a critical realignment occurred, replacing current political arrangements and definitions with new ones, but retaining the individual system of voter participation as was done in the 1932 realignment. The resultant revamping of the individual system of electoral participation would presumably result in bringing more Americans to the polls. That is, even though Americans would still be essentially responsible as individuals for getting themselves to the polls, they would be supplied with a new set of connections and links to the political system that would be more effective in this regard.

The second way would be through the installation of a collectively oriented system of voter participation. This could also happen through a critical realignment, or through an effort on the part of a large block of political forces to reform the system. Either way, it seems likely that it would require more of a conscious social will to move in this direction, since the institutional basis for such a system is not currently present, and the idea of a collective orientation toward voter turnout is not a familiar one in American politics.

What can be said with some assurance is that such a collectively oriented system of voting participation, in which the state and political parties have the burden of responsibility for getting voters to the polls, is likely to be much more effective and stabler than the system we have now. Because it is quite possible we will have the opportunity in the relatively near future to replace the sputtering system of electoral participation we have now with a new one— either because a large enough block of political forces finally sees the necessity for reforming the electoral participation system, or because of the tardy arrival of a real critical realignment—why not take the opportunity to move to the more effective and stabler type of system? If we did, there would probably be fewer turnout puzzles to solve in the future but more voters in the polling booths. It seems like a worthwhile tradeoff.

Appendix: Data Set and Coding of Variables

Selecting the Data Set

Selecting the data set for this study is not a difficult task. This is not because there is an extant data set so unflawed that it is unquestionably the superior choice. Instead, the ease of the task stems from the lack of appropriateness of all data sets save one. This data set is derived from the American National Election Studies (ANES), the same set of surveys used by Abramson and Aldrich, Shaffer, and Cassel and Hill in their analyses of turnout.[1]

The reason why this data set is the only appropriate one is that the ANES taps the full range of characteristics needed to analyze turnout decline, while other data bases do not. The Current Population Survey (CPS), for instance, which is used by Wolfinger and Rosenstone, reports only demographic information on respondents. There are no items of an attitudinal or sociopolitical nature, save for the item on turnout in the previous election. The ANES, in contrast, not only has the basic demographic information needed for the analyses in this study, but also a wide range of questions on attitudes and behaviors of a political nature. This fact makes the ANES far preferable—indeed essential—despite the relatively small number of cases (about 1,500 a year, compared with the 70,000 or so for the CPS).

Overreporting. The ANES, however, is by no means without its drawbacks. The first, and most obvious, is that the dependent

variable, turnout, is considerably overreported in these surveys—
by about fifteen percentage points in most years. Although hardly
desirable, there are several reasons why this problem is not as severe as it might initially appear.

The first is that, despite the consistent overreporting of turnout,
the ANES data do closely parallel real world trends observed in
other sources like election statistics. The ANES data, just as "real
world" statistics do, show that turnout peaked in 1960 and then
declined in every presidential election thereafter, through the one
held in 1980. While the drop in turnout levels recorded by the
ANES surveys is somewhat less than that reported in election statistics (8 percent as opposed to 10 percent), the correlation between the trend in the ANES data and the actual trend is a very
high .98 (Abramson and Aldrich 1982, p. 503). Because the object
of this investigation is to study turnout trends, not predict turnout
in individual years, this is encouraging news.

The second reason is that the aggregate percentages given in
election statistics typically underestimate turnout levels. In other
words, turnout levels in the general population are not really as
low as these statistics imply. This is because these aggregate percentages are usually calculated with a population base that includes millions of people ineligible to vote: aliens, inmates of pris-
ons and mental institutions, and ex-convicts, who cannot vote in
many states. Thus the difference between reported turnout of eligible voters in the ANES surveys and actual turnout of eligible
voters is not as great as it appears at first glance.

The third point salient here is that the ANES surveys will tend
to overestimate turnout, irrespective of the veracity of individual
respondents. This is because the samples are generally restricted
to eligible voters in private households, thereby excluding such
low turnout groups as residents of nursing homes and rooming
houses. Again, this suggests that the observed differences between
reported and actual turnout exaggerate the extent of the problem.

None of the above, however, can be taken to mean that misreporting of voting participation is not a problem with the ANES
data set. Put bluntly, some of the respondents simply do not tell
the truth when asked whether they voted or not (8 to 11 percent,
according to vote validation studies done by those who fielded the

ANES survey). In most cases, this is probably due to the desire of these respondents not to appear socially irresponsible.

Whatever the motivations of individual respondents, the important question then becomes: how serious will be the biases introduced by this misreporting? Fortunately, there are a number of indications that these biases should not be severe for the type of analysis I am attempting. To begin with, misreporting does not appear to be strongly linked to most demographic characteristics (Traugott and Katosh 1979). The one exception is race, where black respondents are roughly twice as likely as whites to say that they voted when they did not. Other than that, misreporting is slightly more common among the very young and the very poor, and more or less randomly distributed among other demographic categories. Because being young, poor, or nonwhite is generally supposed to lower the probability of voting, this should introduce a conservative bias into the effects estimated for these characteristics. In other words, the true effects of age, income, and race (if the direction of these effects is as the received wisdom indicates) will actually be stronger than those discovered by analyzing the ANES data set. This is greatly preferable to a situation in which the bias is not conservative, and nonexistent effects can therefore be estimated.

As for the relation of sociopolitical characteristics to misreporting, this appears to be even less of a problem. According to Abramson and Aldrich (1982), there are negligible differences in the level of overreporting among (white) respondents with varying levels of partisanship and political efficacy. Traugott and Katosh (1979) and Katosh and Traugott (1981) examined a wider range of the attitudinal variables used in the ANES and found no strong relationships between these variables and misreporting.

Of course, none of the points made above prove that there will be no serious biases in analyses produced with this data—although they do indicate that the likelihood of such problems is considerably less than would originally have been supposed. Given this uncertainty, what can be done to compensate for this drawback of the data set? The first, and most obvious, is that where biases are known to exist, these biases should be taken into account when interpreting the results of the data analysis. For in-

stance, the effects estimated for race should be treated with caution, given the much stronger tendency of blacks to misreport voter
participation.

The second possibility is to use the "validated" voting results
that accompanied the ANES in 1964, 1976, and 1980 to check
research findings. This validation was performed by matching a
respondent's self-report of participation with actual voting records
(where possible), and thereby creating a corrected turnout variable. This more accurate report of turnout can thus be used to
assess the viability of controversial or anomalous findings, should
they arise. Of course, to the extent that results are based on an
analysis of data from the entire period, better data for two or
three elections does not provide a good basis for establishing the
validity of research findings. Still the corrected turnout data is a
potentially useful resource, under certain circumstances.

This discussion may be summed up by saying that, despite the
limitations that have been noted, the ANES data set provides the
best—and indeed the only—source for a study that wishes to investigate the role of both demographic and sociopolitical characteristics in turnout decline over the 1960–1980 period. Thus the
logical course of action is to use the ANES data throughout the
research process, while attempting to remain cognizant of its limitations.

Missing Values. The other problem with the data set is hardly
unique to the ANES. This has to with the existence of missing
values on certain cases in the data. There are likely to be a significant number of such cases, given (a) the fact that the analysis
planned is of an extensive, multivariate nature. The larger the
number of variables, the greater the chances that any given case
will have at least one missing value on a variable; and (b) the fact
that some of the variables are attitudinal or sociopolitical. Generally speaking, these variables have more missing value-type responses (especially "don't know") than more objective, demographic measures.

Thus decisions have to be made about how to deal with missing
values. The easiest way is to delete all cases with such values from
the analysis. This is feasible when the number of cases involved is
small, so that their deletion is not likely to affect parameter esti-

mates. When the number of cases is relatively large, however, deletion can seriously affect the reliability of these estimates.

The strategy adopted is therefore designed to maximize the number of cases available for analysis by retaining cases with missing values wherever possible. This entails a threefold strategy. The first part of the strategy is to actually eliminate missing values when the number of such cases (for a given variable) is small—under twenty for each survey year. This should not adversely affect the reliability of estimates.

The second element of the strategy is to recode the missing values into a category to which the missing value response (such as "don't know") can be theoretically linked. An example of this might be a question that asks respondents whether they agree or disagree that the government is responsive to their wishes. A "don't know" response can be viewed as not constituting a positive assessment of government responsiveness as, of course, can a specific disagreement that the government is responsive. The idea, then, would be to combine the negative and "don't know" responses into a single category. This collapsing over categories can then be tested, by means of statistical criteria, to see whether a significant amount of information has been lost through this recoding. If such is not the case, the recoding can legitimately be used in the analysis. This is the general procedure that is used where the theoretical links mentioned above exist.

The third part of the strategy is used when there is no theoretically substantive reason to combine categories, or when such a justification exists but the tests mentioned above are negative. In these instances, the missing values are recoded as the mean value of the variable or into the model category (as is relevant in most cases—see the discussion of categorical versus interval variables in the next section). This procedure, by reducing the variance on a given variable, can attenuate the estimates of that variable's effect, but this is preferable to the problems that would be created by excluding large numbers of cases from the analysis.

To sum up the discussion, there are likely to be a large number of cases in the data set with missing values on one or more variables. Because of this, a strategy has been devised to retain most of these cases in the analysis. Although there are problems with the strategy, it is felt that they are outweighed by the advantages of not having to delete so many cases from the data set.

Coding of Variables: Social Structural Measures

Education. Education was coded as a series of categories, rather than as an interval-level variable, such as years of schooling. This reflects a decision that was made to code variables as categorical wherever there was not a compelling reason to use an alternative method. In this way, meaningful contrasts could be made between the categories coded, in terms of their relationship to the dependent variable. This information is lost when the interval-level assumption is used, so it was felt that making this assumption should generally be avoided.

Categorical variables become unwieldy when too much of this information is retained (i.e., when there are a large number of categories; technically, one could treat every different value of a variable as a separate category—in fact, this is really what is contained within the structure of the data). Thus efforts were made to trim the number of categories down to those that captured the most important and significant contrasts. In the case of education, these categories consisted of less than nine years of education, nine to eleven years, high school graduates, some college, and college graduates.[2]

Occupation and Income. Occupation was coded and treated as a categorical variable. The key categories were found to be housewives, blue-collar workers (including service workers), and a category including white-collar workers and all others. In other words, the only two occupations that were found to make a difference—controlling for education, etc.—to an individual's probability of voting were blue collar and housewife. All others were roughly the same.

Income was coded as a simple dichotomy, between poor and nonpoor, poor being defined as a family income of less than $5,000, in 1960 dollars. This is based on the finding, corroborated by Wolfinger and Rosenstone (1980), that additional income has little independent effect on turnout once a certain minimal threshold in living standards is reached.

Age. Age was also coded and treated as categorical. The key categories were found to be eighteen to twenty-four, twenty-five to twenty-eight, twenty-nine to thirty-two, thirty-three to thirty-six, and thirty-seven or over. The first category, eighteen to twenty-four, contains only twenty-one- to twenty-four-year-olds until 1972, since it was not until that year that eighteen- to twenty-year-olds got the vote. The two groups behave similarly relative to turnout, however, so it was appropriate to put them together in one category.

At the other end of the age spectrum, it was found that there was no significant difference between age groups once the age of thirty-seven had been attained. This is consistent with Wolfinger and Rosenstone's findings concerning the leveling out of the age effect once the young adult years are left behind. It also makes sense theoretically, if the effect of age on turnout is due to the accumulation of basic, cost-reducing political experience. Once a certain level of competence has been attained—which most people presumably will have by the age of thirty-seven—the addition of more experience should make little difference.

Residential Mobility and Marital Status. Residential mobility was dichotomized between those who had moved within two years and those who had not. Continuous residence beyond two years had roughly the same effect, relative to those mobile within that period, no matter how long the length of residence. This makes sense, if the effect of mobility on turnout is due to the necessity for mobile individuals to reabsorb certain start-up costs of voting, as well as develop the links and ties within their community that would encourage participation. Two years should be plenty of time for this to be done. Additional years in the same residence should therefore have little effect.

There is an important problem with the residential mobility variable that should be mentioned here. This problem has its origins in the occasional failure of those who design the ANES to maintain comparability of interview items from one election year to another. In this case, the designers failed to include a question specifically on residential mobility in the 1968 and 1972 surveys. Instead, there is a question on *geographic* mobility—that is, the length of time the respondent has lived in his or her current community. Clearly, there is no reason why the lengths of time measured by the two questions should be identical.

This problem, however, is not as severe as it appears at first glance. Although it is true that the lengths of time will not necessarily be identical, it is also true that the length of time at current residence will always be less than or equal to the length of time in current community. In other words, someone who has been geographically mobile within two years is certain to have been residentially mobile within that period. Thus the geographic mobility variable may be treated as a residential mobility variable, with certain obvious limitations.

The first limitation is that many people who are residentially mobile will not be coded as being so, since they were not geographically mobile as well during the two-year time period. Thus the population proportions for being mobile in 1968 and 1972 will considerably underestimate the true population proportions. The second limitation flows from the first. Because the 1968 and 1972 mobility variables code some mobile individuals as nonmobile, this should attenuate the effect of mobility in those years, since the contrast between the two categories will be lessened.

These limitations, while not desirable, can be dealt with. Population proportions for 1968 and 1972 can be estimated through interpolation, based on the figures for other years. And the problem posed by the possible attenuation of the mobility effect in 1968 and 1972 will be mitigated by using the entire pooled data set to estimate this effect. In addition, interactions between mobility and year can be examined to determine whether the attenuation is severe (this would be suggested by strong interaction effects in 1968 and 1972). While these correctives and checks are hardly foolproof, using them, and the mobility data to which they are linked, is preferable to eliminating this variable from the analysis.

The other characteristic mentioned earlier, marital status, was dichotomized between those married and living with spouse, and those who were not. This latter category includes those never married, as well as those divorced, separated, or widowed. There was found to be little difference among these four groups in terms of their relationship to turnout, a fact that makes sense if the key aspect of marital status is the link to a spouse, and the personal interactions/community "rootedness" that it engenders. Thus the particular manner in which individuals lack a spousal link—never married, divorced, etc.—should not be salient. The lack of this link is the important thing, and this is reflected in the dichotomization just described.

Race, Region, and Sex. These three characteristics were coded as dichotomies: white and nonwhite, South and non-South, male and female. These are the standard categorizations used for these variables in analyses of turnout and were found to be useful here as well.[3]

Coding of Variables: Sociopolitical Measures

Partisanship. Partisanship measures the extent to which an individual identifies with one of the political parties—or lacks such an identification. In this case, it summarizes the responses to the questions shown in Table A-1.

A three-point interval scale (0,1,2) was used to represent the partisanship variable. This is because (a) it is the same type of scale used by Abramson and Aldrich, thereby enhancing comparability of results; and (b) a comparison of this scale with a categorical treatment of the variable revealed that the loss of information from fitting fewer parameters was not substantial.

The scale was constructed in the following way. The lowest category groups pure independents together with those who described themselves as apolitical or supporters of minor parties. These groups were found to have a similarly low proclivity to vote, so they were put together in a single category. The middle category groups weak partisans with "independent leaners." The last, and highest, category contains self-described strong partisans, since they were found to have a distinctly higher propensity to vote than the weak partisans/independent leaners.

Political Efficacy. The two questions on which the efficacy scale is based are shown in Table A-1. They solicit respondents' opinions about whether they have influence over the government and public officials. These two questions have been shown to have both face and construct validity (House and Mason 1975), as well as scaling reliably (Mason, House, and Martin 1981). Following the lead of previous researchers on turnout decline (Shaffer, Abramson and Aldrich), a three-point interval scale (0,1,2) was used, going from low to medium to high efficacy. Those who disagreed with neither statement were scored as low, those who disagreed

Table A-1
Questions for Sociopolitical Variables

POLITICAL EFFICACY
(agree or disagree)

1. People like me don't have any say about what the government does.

2. I don't think public officials care much what people like me think.

PARTISANSHIP
(summary of responses)

A. Generally speaking, do you usually think of yourself as a Republican, a Democrat, an independent, or what?

(for Democratic and Republican partisans)
B. Would you call yourself a strong Republican (Democrat) or a not very strong Republican (Democrat)?

(for independents, no preference, other)
C. Do you think of yourself as closer to the Republican Party or to the Democratic Party?

CAMPAIGN NEWSPAPER READING
(summary of responses)

1960, 1964, 1968, 1976, 1980
A1. Did you read about the campaign in any of the newspapers?

1972
A2. Did you read much about the campaign in any of the newspapers?

(if yes)
1960, 1964, 1968, 1972, 1976
B1. How much did you read newspaper articles about the election--regularly, often, from time to time, or just once in a great while?

1980
B2. How many newspaper articles did you read about the campaign--would say you read a good many, several, or just one or two?

---

with only one were scored medium, and those who disagreed with both were designated high.[4]

Campaign Newspaper Reading. This variable is based on responses to the questions shown in Table A-1. The responses were divided into three categories: those reading many articles, those reading only some, and those reading none. These were the key distinctions to be made among the responses, in terms of behavioral relationship to turnout. The three groupings were treated categorically and were represented by two dummy variables, one for some articles read and one for many articles. No articles read was the reference category.

This question was not asked in precisely the same way in all years, as is detailed in Table A-1. Specifically, in 1972 the wording of the first question was, "Did you read *much* about . . . " (emphasis added), rather than, "Did you read about . . . ," as it was in all other years. It is possible that this resulted in more "no" responses (coded as "no articles") than would have been the case had the question been phrased as it usually was. This may have contributed to the strikingly large proportion in this category in 1972 (see Table 1-1).

There is no reason, however, to believe that the proportion of responses coded as "many articles" (regularly, often) should have been seriously affected by this inconsistency. This is because it is unlikely that someone who regularly/often read articles about the campaign would say "no" when asked if they had read much about the election in the papers, and thus be filtered out of the second question. Because the "many articles" proportion also fell drastically in this year (Table 1-1), this suggests that the 1968–1972 decline in campaign newspaper reading was nevertheless substantial, if exaggerated in the "no articles" category.

It is also possible that the different wording for the second question in 1980 resulted in some overestimation of the "some articles" category. This is because some people who might have said "often" to the question, as phrased in previous years, and thus been classified as "many articles," replied "several" with the 1980 wording, and thus were classified as "some articles." However, because it seems likely that most respondents who read the newspapers often about the election would consider that amount "a good many," the extent of this overestimation should be small—

if it exists at all. (Note: Questions and coding for variable in 1984 are identical to that in 1980.)

These problems, while not desirable, are not serious enough to warrant excluding the variable from analysis. Instead, it is preferable to use the variable but keep in mind possible effects of these wording discrepancies. In addition, the newspaper reading variable can be checked for effect changes in the anomalous years, to see if the distortions are severe enough to have an effect on parameter estimates.

Notes

1. The specific part of the survey used in their studies and my own is the preelection/postelection sample. This sample interviews the same set of respondents both before and after the election. It has been taken every year the ANES survey has been taken.

2. There were few cases with missing values on this variable, so those cases were simply omitted from the analysis. A similar situation obtained for race, region, and sex. For all other social structural variables, missing values were coded as the modal category. The rationale for these procedures was detailed in the previous section of the Appendix.

3. A word should be said about the race dichotomization. It is claimed by some investigators that the effects of being nonwhite are not uniform across nonwhite groups. Specifically, it is advised that the effects of being black and Hispanic be disaggregated (Wolfinger and Rosenstone 1980, pp. 90–93). In my analyses, however, I did not find important differences between nonwhite groups. In any event, the size of my data set makes it difficult to perform reliable analyses of small subpopulations.

4. Missing values on these questions were "don't knows." It was felt that these were meaningful responses to the questions, which, while not agreement, represented a lack of disagreement. Given this and the fact that there was little difference in relationship to turnout between this response and "agree," the missing values were coded, along with "agree," as a single category ("did not disagree").

The other two sociopolitical variables were handled differently. For partisanship, there were few actual missing values (as opposed to "apolitical," "other," etc.), so these cases were simply eliminated from the analysis. For newspaper reading, missing values were coded as the modal category.

References

Abramson, Paul, and John Aldrich. "The Decline of Electoral Participation in America." *American Political Science Review* 76 (1982): 502–21.

Aldrich, John, and Dennis Simon. "Turnout in American National Elections." *Research in Micropolitics* 1 (1986): 271–301.

Almond, Gabriel, and Sidney Verba. *The Civic Culture.* Princeton, N.J.: Princeton University Press, 1963.

Americans for Civic Participation. "Project Vote." Brochure, 1984.

Andersen, Kristi. *The Creation of a Democratic Majority.* Chicago: University of Chicago Press, 1979.

Asher, Herbert. *Presidential Elections and American Politics.* Homewood, Ill.: Dorsey Press, 1980.

Baker, R. J., and J. A. Nelder. *The GLIM System: Generalized Linear Modelling.* Oxford, England: Royal Statistical Society, 1978.

Bartzel, Yoram, and Eugene Silverberg. "Is the Act of Voting Rational?" *Public Choice* 16 (Fall 1973).

Berelson, Bernard, Paul Lazarsfeld, and William McPhee. *Voting.* Chicago: University of Chicago Press, 1954.

Bishop, Yvonne M. M., Stephen E. Feinberg, and Paul W. Holland. *Discrete Multivariate Analysis: Theory and Practice.* Cambridge, Mass.: MIT Press, 1975.

Blumenthal, Sidney. *The Permanent Campaign.* Boston: Beacon Press, 1980.

Blumenthal, Sidney. "Media and Illusion in the Permanent Campaign." *Working Papers* 9 (1982): 46–52.

Boyd, Richard. "Decline of U.S. Voter Turnout: Structural Explanations." *American Politics Quarterly* 9 (1981): 123–59.

Brody, Richard. "The Puzzle of Political Participation." In *The New American Political System*, edited by Anthony King. Washington, D.C.: American Enterprise Institute, 1978.

Brody, Richard, and Benjamin Page. "Indifference, Alienation and Rational Decisions: The Effects of Candidate Evaluations on Turnout and the Vote." *Public Choice* 15 (Summer 1973).

Brownell, Blaine, and Warren Stickle. *Bosses and Reformers: Urban Politics in America, 1880–1920*. Boston: Houghton Mifflin, 1973.

Brunk, Gregory C. "The Impact of Rational Participation Models on Voting Attitudes." *Public Choice* 35 (1980).

Burnham, Walter Dean. *Critical Elections and the Mainsprings of American Politics*. New York: W. W. Norton, 1970.

Burnham, Walter Dean. "The U.S.: The Politics of Heterogeneity." In *Electoral Behavior*, edited by Richard Rose. New York: Macmillan, 1974.

Burnham, Walter Dean. "American Politics in the Seventies—Beyond Party." In *The Future of Political Parties*, edited by Louis Maisel and Paul Sacks. Beverly Hill, Calif.: Sage, 1975.

Burnham, Walter Dean. *The Current Crisis in American Politics*. New York: Oxford University Press, 1982.

Burstein, Paul. "Social Structure and Individual Political Participation in Five Countries." *American Journal of Sociology* 77 (1971): 1087–1110.

Campbell, Angus, Philip Converse, Warren Miller, and Donald Stokes. *The American Voter*. New York: John Wiley & Sons, 1960.

Campbell, B. A. *The American Electorate*. New York: Holt, Rinehart & Winston, 1979.

Carter, James. "Crisis of Confidence." Presidential speech, 1976.

Cassel, Carol A., and David Hill. "Explanations of Turnout Decline: A Multivariate Test." *American Politics Quarterly* 9 (1981): 181–95.

Cassel, Carol A., and David Hill. "Comment on Abramson and Aldrich." *American Political Science Review* 77 (1983): 1011–12.

Cavanaugh, Thomas E. "Changes in American Voter Turnout, 1964–1976." *Political Science Quarterly* (Spring 1981).

Chagall, David. *The New Kingmakers*. New York: Harcourt, Brace, Jovanovich, 1981.

Chambers, William Nisbet, and Walter Dean Burnham. *The American Party Systems*. New York: Oxford University Press, 1967.

Clotfelter, J., and C. L. Prysby. *Political Choices: A Study of Elections and Voters*. New York: Holt, Rinehart & Winston, 1980.

Committee for the Study of the American Electorate. "Turnout Increases Slightly in 1984." Press release, November 9, 1984.

Converse, Phillip. *Dynamics of Party Identification*. Beverly Hills, Calif.: Sage, 1976.

Cyr, A. Bruce. "The Calculus of Voting Reconsidered." *Public Opinion Quarterly* 39 (1975): 19–38.

Downs, Anthony. *Economic Theory of Democracy*. New York: Harper & Bros., 1957.

Duverger, Maurice. *Political Parties*. New York: John Wiley & Sons, 1973.

Elster, Jon. *Ulysses and the Sirens*. New York: Cambridge University Press, 1979.

Erikson, Robert S. "Why Do People Vote?: Because They Are Registered." Paper read at National Science Foundation Conference on Voter Turnout, San Diego, May 16–19, 1979.

Ferejohn, J. A., and M. P. Fiorina. "The Paradox of Voting: A Decision-Theoretic Analysis." *American Political Science Review* 68 (1974): 525–36.

Filer, John, and Lawrence W. Kenny. "Voter Turnout and the Benefits of Voting." *Public Choice* 33 (1980).

Frey, Bruno S. "Why Do High Income People Participate in Elections?" *Public Choice* (Fall 1971): 101–5.

Glenn, Norval. *Cohort Analysis*. Beverly Hills, Calif.: Sage, 1977.

Graber, Doris. "Press and TV as Opinion Resources in Presidential Campaigns." *Public Opinion Quarterly* 40 (Fall 1976): 285–303.

Hadley, Arthur. *The Empty Polling Booth*. Englewood Cliffs, N.J.: Prentice-Hall, 1978.

Hamilton, Richard. *Class and Politics in the United States*. New York: John Wiley & Sons, 1972.

Hannushek, Eric A., and John E. Jackson. *Statistical Methods for Social Scientists*. New York: Academic Press, 1977.

Hofstadter, Richard, William Miller, and Daniel Aaron. *The United States: The History of a Republic*. Englewood Cliffs, N.J.: Prentice-Hall, 1967.

House, James, and William Mason. "Political Alienation in America, 1952–1968." *American Sociological Review* 40 (1975): 123–47.

Hout, Michael, and David Knoke. "Change in Voting Turnout, 1952–1972." *Public Opinion Quarterly* 39 (Spring 1975): 52–68.

Judis, John. "No Place to Go: The Steady Rise of the Non-Voters' Party." *The Progressive* 44 (October 1980): 18–21.

Katosh, John, and Michael Traugott. "The Consequences of Validated and Self-reported Voting Measures." *Public Opinion Quarterly* 45 (1981): 519–35.

Key, V. O. *Southern Politics in State and Nation.* New York: Alfred Knopf, 1949.

Kornhauser, William. *The Politics of Mass Society.* New York: Free Press, 1959.

Kraus, Sidney, and Dennis Davis. *The Effects of Mass Communications on Political Behavior.* University Park, Penn.: Pennsylvania State University Press, 1976.

Lipset, Seymour Martin. *Political Man.* Baltimore: Johns Hopkins University Press, 1981.

Lipset, Seymour Martin, and Stein Rokkan. *Party Systems and Voter Alignment.* New York: Free Press, 1967.

Lipset, Seymour Martin, and William Schneider. *The Confidence Gap.* New York: Free Press, 1983.

Mare, Robert. Lectures on analysis of categorical data. University of Wisconsin, Spring 1983.

Mason, William, James House, and Steven Martin. "Dimensions of Political Alienation in America: Theoretical and Empirical." Unpublished manuscript, University of Michigan, 1981.

Merriam, Charles, and Harold Gosnell. *Non-Voting.* Chicago: University of Chicago Press, 1924.

Milbraith, Lester. *Political Participation.* Chicago: Rand-McNally, 1965.

Miller, Warren E., Arthur Miller, and Edward Schneider. *American National Election Studies Sourcebook, 1952–1978.* Cambridge, Mass.: Harvard University Press, 1980.

Nelson, Candice, Bruce Eith, Elizabeth Orr, Mark C. Westyle, Raymond Wolfinger, and David Magleby. Unpublished paper delivered at American Political Science Association convention, Chicago, 1983.

Nie, Norman, Sidney Verba, and John Petrocik. *The Changing American Voter.* Cambridge, Mass.: Harvard University Press, 1976.

Niemi, Richard. "Costs of Voting and Non-Voting." *Public Choice* 27 (Fall 1976).

Olson, Mancur. *Logic of Collective Action.* Cambridge, Mass.: Harvard University Press, 1965.

Osborne, David. "Registration Boomerang." *New Republic,* February 25, 1985: 14–16.

Perlez, Jane. "Does Voter Registration Cut Two Ways?" *New York Times,* April 13, 1984.

Petrocik, John R. "Voter Turnout and Electoral Oscillation." *American Politics Quarterly* 9 (1981): 161–80.

Prisuta, Robert H. "Mass Media Exposure and Political Behavior." *Educational Broadcasting Review* 7 (1973): 167–73.

Przeworski, Adam. "Institutionalization of Voting Patterns, or, is Mobilization the Source of Decay." *American Political Science Review* 69 (1975).

Ranney, Austin. *Channels of Power*. New York: Basic Books, 1983.

Reiter, Howard L. "Why Is Turnout Down?" *Public Opinion Quarterly* 43 (1979): 297–311.

Riker, William, and Peter Ordeshook. "A Theory of the Calculus of Voting." *American Political Science Review* 62 (1968): 25–42.

Rogers, Joel. "The Politics of Voter Registration." *The Nation*, July 21, 1984, pp. 34, 45–51.

Rollenhagen, Richard E. "Exploring Variation in Concern About the Outcome of Presidential Elections." Unpublished paper, Michigan State University, 1981.

Rosenstone, Steven. "Economic Adversity and Voter Turnout." *American Journal of Political Science* 26 (1982): 25–46.

Sabato, Lawrence. *The Rise of Political Consultants*. New York: Basic Books, 1981.

Santi, Lawrence. "The Changing Demographic Bases of Electoral Participation, 1964–1976." Unpublished paper, Reed College, 1982.

Settle, Russel F., and Buran A. Abrams. "The Determinants of Voter Participation: A More General Model." *Public Choice* 27 (Fall 1976).

Shaffer, Robert. "A Multivariate Explanation of Decreasing Turnout in Presidential Elections, 1960–1976." *American Journal of Political Science* 25 (1981): 68–95.

Silberman, Jon, and Gary Burden. "Rational Behavior Theory of Voting Participation: Evidence from Congressional Elections." *Public Choice* 23 (Fall 1975).

Stevenson, Robert. "The Uses and Non-Uses of Television News." Paper delivered at the Annual Meeting of the International Society of Political Psychology, New York, September 1978.

Thurow, Lester. *Zero Sum Society*. New York: Penguin Books, 1981.

Tingsten, Herbert. *Political Behavior*. London: P. S. King, 1937.

Tollison, R. D., and T. D. Willett. "Some Simple Economies of Voting and Non-Voting." *Public Choice* 16 (Fall 1973).

Traugott, Michael, and John Katosh. "Response Validity in Surveys of Voting Behavior." *Public Opinion Quarterly* 43 (1979): 359–77.

Verba, Sidney, and Norman Nie. *Participation in America*. New York: Harper & Row, 1972.

Walsh, Joan. "Gender Gap." *In These Times*, June 13, 1984, pp. 7–12.

Weinstein, James. *Corporate Ideal in the Liberal State*. Boston: Beacon Press, 1971.

Weibe, Robert. *Search for Order, 1877–1920*. New York: Hill & Wang, 1967.

Wolfinger, Raymond, and Steven Rosenstone. *Who Votes?* New Haven, Conn.: Yale University Press, 1980.

Wright, James D. *Dissent of the Governed*. New York: Academic Press, 1976.

Index

About the Author

RUY A. TEIXEIRA is a Senior Analyst specializing in income security, education, and survey research for Abt Associates, Inc. His articles have been published in the *American Journal of Sociology, American Journal of Education,* and *Public Opinion.* He received a Ph.D. in Sociology at the University of Wisconsin in 1984.